FIERY HOPE

Best wishes!

Eveline MacDougall

Fiery Hope

Building community with the Amandla Chorus

Eveline MacDougall

Haley's
Athol, Massachusetts

Copy edited by Debra Ellis.
Proof read by Richard Bruno.

Photos from the collection of Eveline MacDougall
unless otherwise credited.

Cover photo by Mary Newton Rose.
Photo of Eveline in About the Author section by Paul Franz.

Haley's
488 South Main Street
Athol, MA 01331
haley.antique@verizon.net

Names: MacDougall, Eveline, 1964- author.
Title: Fiery hope : building community with the Amandla chorus / Eveline MacDougall.
Description: Athol : Haley's, 2019. | Summary: "A retrospective view of the social justice chorus, Amandla as it evolves to Fiery Hope under the direction of Eveline MacDougall, the author. With autobiographical information about the author. From schoolhouse to jailhouse, with performances advised by Pete Seeger and with and for Nelson Mandela, Malala Yousafzai, and Jane Sapp, Amandla-now Fiery Hope-strives to raise consciousness while offering world music and songs about peace"-- Provided by publisher.
Identifiers: LCCN 2019041066 | ISBN 9781948380102 (trade paperback)
Subjects: LCSH: MacDougall, Eveline, 1964- | Amandla Chorus | Fiery Hope (Choral ensemble) | Choral conductors--United States--Biogaphy. | Choral music--Social aspects. | Choral music--Political aspects. | Social justice.
Classification: LCC ML422.M33 A3 2019 | DDC 782.506--dc23
LC record available at https://lccn.loc.gov/2019041066

In loving memory of

Ursula Marie Snow,

who lived her life with passion and peace

photo by Yael Rosenbloom

Ursula Marie Snow

Let's sing our way out of this.
—Isabel Fraire

Our own pulse beats in every stranger's throat.
—Barbara Deming

*When the power of love overcomes the love of power,
the world will know peace.*
—Jimi Hendrix

contents

photographs

Powerful Song

an introduction by Eveline MacDougall

A big surprise awaited me because, as a child, I didn't know that music could change lives. I didn't know that many different kinds of music existed.

I knew well the classical music my family played and listened to at home, church, school, and concerts. I also knew the raucous music of Québec, where most of my family lived, but my parents did not consider what they called silly music worthy of the respect they reserved for dead European composers.

A woodwind player, Dad performed in ensembles and taught music lessons in public schools. The sounds of Mom's piano students filled our home when I returned from school each day.

I hadn't yet learned songs that allow people to give voice to laments and dreams. I hadn't heard about songs that move hearts and lead to political change. As a child, I had no conscious knowledge of such songs.

Still, a recurring dream puzzled me the year I turned six: I stood before a group of people I didn't recognize and waved my hands as though directing musicians. The peoples' faces glowed with loving determination as they moved their lips, yet I heard no sound.

The first time I had the dream, I awoke feeling unsettled. The dream's silence mystified me. I didn't understand why the strangers looked expectantly to me. As the dream recurred over several months, my experience of it shifted from unsettling to peaceful. I grew to anticipate joy at seeing the soundless singers' faces glow with delight.

I wondered if they were my ancestors. My parents came from very different backgrounds, and I frequently mused: *Who am I? Where should I live when I grow up – Daddy's country or Mama's?*

My mother, Céline, the youngest in a large family, was born in a Québécois village in 1932. Céline's family lived without running water until she turned seventeen and their home did not have electricity until she was well into her twenties.

A few years after acquiring a flush toilet, Céline and her sister-in-law Denise flattened the old outhouse. They knew their rebellion would anger my grandfather, since he'd insisted on keeping it as a storage shed. "He hated change of any kind," my mother told me decades later. The young women dared step out of line in order to erase what they saw as evidence of backwardness.

When in my early twenties I chose to live with friends in a cabin without running water or electricity, Mom smiled and shook her head. She reacted with similar sanguine acceptance fifteen years later when I gave my car away and decided to travel mostly by foot and bicycle, an experiment that stretched to fourteen years. Céline grew up with horses powering work and providing transportation. When she had a chance as a teen to ride in an uncle's new car, she saw it as the height of progress.

My mother accepts my choices despite priding herself in having modernized. She left behind the need to break ice in the wash basin in order to wash her face but cheers me on as I navigate an era that strikes me as overly mechanized and disconnected from the realities of living on earth.

My father, Bruce, was born in Brooklyn in 1931, yet my urban parent shared with me the joys of mountain climbing, gardening, and geology. He grew up bristling under the expectations of his mother, a high school teacher, and his father, a *New York Times* man. Bruce's wide-ranging interests, including music and world travel, led him to defy his parents' plan that their eldest child pursue a career in chemistry.

Dad shared many interests with his four children, and I yearned to visit and learn from many cultures as he did. I imagined passport stamp marks from around the world but later relinquished that plan after learning about the amount of fuel required to lift an airplane. I felt called to use fewer resources in a world stressed by environmental and political factors.

Initially, I hoped the impulse would pass, but it grew stronger. I miss out on certain adventures, but I have made my peace. I say "bon voyage" to friends who travel for work, to visit family, or to follow their callings. Most of my relatives live in Québec and the northeastern US, so I can keep my travel fairly local from my home base of western Massachusetts.

Before I reached second grade, my dream of silent singers stopped. I made it through elementary school and entered my anxiety-laden adolescence. I forgot about the dream.

At twenty-five years old, with two years of choral directing under my belt, I had the dream once more. I finally heard the singers! I didn't understand the lyrics, but the song's harmonies thrilled me as did my gut feeling that— judging by their shining faces and upraised fists— they sang for freedom and justice.

I awoke feeling tingly. *How could I have forgotten for nearly two decades that I had a similar dream as a child?*

The beautiful classical music that saturated my childhood contains no overt messages of community building or resistance to tyranny. I had no context for social-justice music. Perhaps that's why I couldn't hear the singers when, as a child, I had the dream.

Learning about social-justice music changed my life in astounding ways. A powerful song brought me into the presence of Nelson Mandela shortly after he was released from decades in South African prisons. Music of struggle and celebration led to collaborations with the activist songwriter Pete Seeger as well with the Nobel laureate Malala Yousafzai and her delightful father.

Music of freedom and hope brought me to New York State's largest maximum-security prison, to dusty homeless shelters, overheated trauma wards, and remote rehab units. Music of healing and grace brought me face-to-face with anguished survivors of sexual abuse and domestic violence.

Has my dream come true? Yes and no. Each time I direct the social-justice chorus I founded in 1988, I experience deep joy similar to how I felt at age six during the dream. I'll always love the Zulu name Amandla, meaning power, bestowed upon us by a South African member. That part of my dream came true.

On the other hand, I continue to learn that the truest forms of power can't emerge until we make monumental changes as a human family. The nation where my family moved just before I was born may soar on lofty concepts, yet those concepts will not come to life until people who look like me learn to joyfully and willingly relinquish privileges, limit our consumption, and share resources in favor of greater peace for all. Sadly, that part of my dream has not yet materialized.

I live a waking dream of singing with others to open hearts. But I've learned that I must always start by educating and changing myself. Ongoing lessons prod me to examine my actions and search for ways to live more justly.

So, with fiery hope, I travel the world through song and invite readers to come along.

Music as a way of Life

I led a musical double life from the start. Before my third birthday, I loved mimicking recordings and making up my own songs at the piano. Yet I loathed recitals, auditions, and awards ceremonies, even when I won a little prize issued by the piano teachers' guild called the Felix Mendelssohn Award. At age ten, winning actually made me feel worse.

A few months later, I read in a music history magazine that Mendelssohn's sister, Fanny, composed music as skillfully as did Felix, even giving him pointers. The siblings were close, but apparently Felix discouraged his sister from publishing her work.

I set the article down and walked outdoors to throw my Mendelssohn Award into a creek. I hadn't yet learned about feminism, but I knew about fairness.

The narrow musical world of applause and disapproval seemed galaxies away from my favorite activities of noodling on the fiddle or singing in my tree fort. My love-hate relationship with music deteriorated further during my teens as I witnessed my parents' struggle to survive.

My mother worked at home teaching thirty piano lessons each

Eveline's mother,
Céline Janelle,
the first in her family
to graduate from college

Eveline's father, Bruce, Robert Bruce MacDougall

week as well as classes in her native French. Yet she somehow managed to serve dinner made from scratch every single evening at exactly six o'clock, including sumptuous desserts. I can't fathom how she ran our zany household so efficiently in addition to her paid and volunteer work. When I took a course about feminism in college, I recognized my mother as an unsung hero.

My father played double-reed instruments including oboe, English horn, and oboe d'amore with symphonies and chamber groups. In the early 1960s, he held the position of principal oboist in the Québec Symphony but lost his job due to political unrest. The symphony expelled all players, including my father, who did not speak French as their first language.

Considering the history of marginalized French speakers in Canada, I sympathize with those who wish to preserve and defend the French language in Québec. I also understand the point of view of those excluded.

Given my parents' circumstances, the ouster distressed them. They loved living in Québec City, where they began their married life and welcomed their first child. When they realized the potential limits of my father's employment in French-speaking Canada, they decided to move to the States and start over.

After we settled just over the border, we often traveled north to visit our large extended family, whose last names included Janelle, St. Onge, and Bourgeois. Each time we re-entered the States, Mom pulled out her green card, issued by the Commissioner of Immigration and Naturalization. The fine print fascinated and scared me: "You are required to have

Felix Rajotte, the bride's father; Eveline Rajotte, the bride; Elphège Janelle, the groom; and Athanase Janelle, groom's father, from left, on the wedding day in 1916 of Eveline's maternal grandparents in the farming village of St. Germain de Grantham, Québec

Robert MacDougall and Evelyn Parker, Eveline's paternal grandparents, in 1930

Eveline's parents on their June 27, 1960, wedding day in St. Germain, Québec.
When their families met that day but did not share a language,
they could not converse beyond saying "Hello."

Eveline's mother's United States Permanent Resident's Card or green card

this card with you at all times." It specified that my mother was "admitted to the United States as an immigrant." I always held my breath at the border, wondering what we'd do if the customs officials denied my mother entrance to the US. That baseless fear nonetheless haunted my dreams.

When I hear of immigrants and refugees the world over, I think about the children. A particular heartache distresses me as I imagine kids living with anxiety far greater than what I experienced.

Eveline grew up listening to her father's Vermont-based woodwind quintet, from left, Mary Lou Cox, Bruce MacDougall, David Racuson, Earl North, and Fran Cardillo.

Eveline's parents playing duets, top, 1961, and
Eveline and her eldest brother, Andrew, playing duets in 1967

Dad opted for steady work as a public-school music teacher but dreaded working with kids who weren't serious about music. Fortunately, he also found a position as principal oboist with the Vermont Symphony. He also formed a quintet. He felt happy while rehearsing and performing with professionals but disliked the daily grind of teaching. Dad's highs were stratospheric and his lows were dreadful. Yet through it all, music remained his path.

I had no idea I'd grow up to combine music with social-justice work, but the signs appeared everywhere. Directing a chorus is a joyful, challenging adventure, allowing me to explore and enjoy music while leaving most of the negative aspects behind.

My work history is varied and hodge-podge since entering the workforce at nineteen. I prefer being my own boss, but I am willing on occasion to toil for others who respect the value of a good worker.

I liked working on construction crews, waiting on tables, and filling potholes. I enjoy substitute teaching and freelance editing. I learned a lot while farming, touring with political theater troupes, cashiering at food co-ops, and caring for toddlers. Thanks to my parents, I always have options like teaching piano or performing with ensembles.

I felt grown up having my own office at the age of twenty while working as communications director for the Student Association of the State University (SASU) in Albany, New York. I appreciated receiving modest employment benefits but found that office work is not for me. Since 1985, I've received no paid vacations, paid sick days, medical insurance, or other perks related to mainstream employment.

In describing how my choices relate to my work, I do not suggest that my preferences are right for everyone.

A dreamy child, I gravitated toward books, music, and the rhythms of two cultures and two languages. The strong opinions and deeply held values of my American father and French-Canadian mother affected me greatly. My parents took the Gospels literally, viewing wealth and privilege as sins that result in poverty for those less powerful.

Some of my uncommon choices came with a sense of righteousness, but the smugness of my youth evolved to understanding that each of us arrives at decisions and lifestyles on our own paths.

My avoidance of air travel except in emergencies, foregoing various forms of technology, and refusing to pay income taxes in order to protest the funding of wars feel right to me, but I don't believe there's only one way to do things.

Friends warn that my elder years will be precarious without a safety net, and I know they're right. But I'm not inspired to make decisions based purely on pragmatism or economics. Some say I'm naïve, but I trust that if I do what I love, it will come out right.

I choose this life because I love variety and freedom. Directing a social-justice chorus provides variety year after year.

While my choral director income is low in terms of dollars, I reap enormous "soul payment." Still, at the end of each season, I ask myself: *Can I afford to keep doing this? Should I get a regular job?*

One thing that helps me decide is to turn the pages of scrapbooks while recalling vignettes that buoyed my spirit, broke my heart, and gave me a front-row seat to living on planet earth in the late twentieth and early twenty-first centuries. Each year since 1988, I renew my decision that I wouldn't trade this life for anything.

Amandla begins : 1988

I hoped for enough participants to sing four-part harmonies, but given the short notice, I knew it was a long shot. I feared few people would show up on a frigid January day in a tiny New England town for the sole purpose of singing South African freedom songs.

Forty people arrived, exceeding my hopes. Many kept their coats on in the small, drafty building formerly used as a church.

Weeks earlier, Rosie Heidkamp suggested I offer an informal workshop. She lived in South Africa as a child and retained a deep fondness for that country's rich harmonies. We hoped to raise awareness about anti-apartheid activism while plugging into unparalleled musical energy.

Preparing to teach parts for "Freedom Is Coming," I said, "Sopranos, you sing the lead of the call and response."

And we were off. What was billed as a one-time session blossomed into a project that's grown and changed since 1988, taking me and my cohorts into the company of thousands of people in public and private venues as well as forgotten or out-of-the-way places.

A South African friend suggested we call our new group Amandla, the Zulu word for power, found in many freedom songs from that part of the world.

The Amandla Chorus was born that day in Wendell, yet its roots can also be traced to Noonday Farm, the cooperative volunteer enterprise in nearby Winchendon Springs where I first sang South African freedom songs in 1986.

The first inklings of the Amandla Chorus also include the day in 1985 when I walked from my office in Albany to a protest organized by the indomitable Dr. Boji Jordan. I first heard South African protest songs at a small event in front of a jewelry store selling South African Krugerrand coins. Several South African

poster announcing Wendell, Massachusetts, session that led to formation of Amandla

activists shared songs from their homeland to publicize the importance of boycotting businesses that lined the pockets of the racist South African regime. I lived and breathed music all my life, but those were the most gorgeous harmonies I'd ever heard.

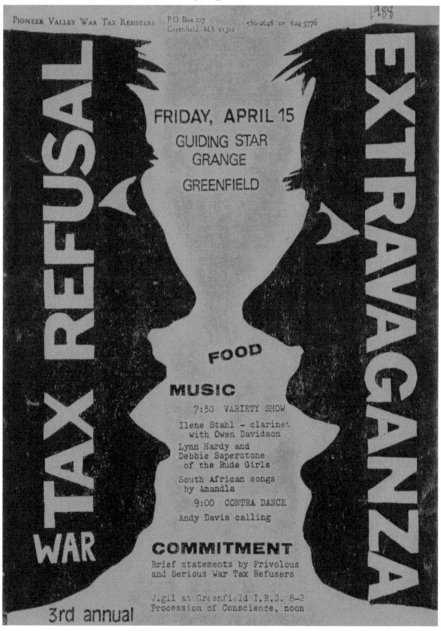

Amandla's first gig, advertised with a poster created by Marilyn Andrews

My parents inhabited a world steeped in classical music. That path led to disappointments and bruised them economically, yet their passion never waned for the music or for each other.

I also witnessed my parents' dedication to boycotts, protests, and social justice. I was a small child during the Vietnam War, but I recall my father weeping and raging about headlines, politics, and body counts. My mother similarly abhorred war and violence.

Céline Janelle and Bruce MacDougall came from two very different places, languages, religions, and cultures.

My mother, the youngest of many children (eight of whom survived to adulthood), grew up on a dairy farm in the tiny Québécois village of St. Germain de Grantham. My staunchly Catholic, French-speaking grandparents, Eveline and Elphège, worked hard as subsistence farmers.

My father was born in Brooklyn to Evelyn, a Barnard-educated teacher of English, and Robert, who worked for the *New York Times* for many years and later for an oil-company newspaper in Oklahoma.

My parents met in 1958 in Regina, Saskatchewan, where my father taught music for a year, and where my mother visited her sister for an extended stay after the death of their mother. Their families met only once, at my parents' Monday morning wedding in St. Germain on June 27, 1960. My paternal grandparents resigned themselves to the fact that this strange rite legalized the union of the improbable couple who would become my parents. In their late twenties, Céline and Bruce began a new story. United by a deep love of music and the arts, they imbued my three brothers and me with values that led to our rather unconventional lives.

Even in rare free moments, my parents immersed themselves in music, attending concerts, listening to classical music on the radio, and rehearsing our family orchestra.

Naughty hilarity filled practice sessions as my eldest brother, Andrew (bassoon), and I (violin) cracked each other up. Our younger brothers, Robert (clarinet) and Ian (drum), did their best under the kind but exacting tutelage of our parents. Dad played a variety of woodwinds, and Mom played the flute. Though not intending to follow in my parents' footsteps, I learned by osmosis skills related to directing a musical group.

We performed at nursing homes, churches, and birthday parties. I rolled my eyes, but secretly I loved collaborating with other musicians, even if they were my parents and bratty brothers. Yet witnessing my parents' long hours and low pay strengthened my resolve to pursue a different career. I could not have predicted that I, too, would spend my days and years immersed in music.

I had a lot of growing up to do when I began directing a large chorus at the age of twenty-three. Singers in those early years witnessed my awkward evolutions. I took certain things too seriously while handling other matters with insufficient wisdom. I don't blame anyone who left in favor of finding a chorus led by a more seasoned grown-up. I'm grateful to those who felt able to stick with it, displaying great patience.

Like a freedom song, our chorus has energy and purpose far bigger than any one person. Within months of our first session, an organizer from Traprock Center for Peace and Justice invited us to open a benefit concert featuring the folk singer Tom Paxton.

The Amherst High School auditorium was packed on that steamy June evening in 1988. As we finished our set, a young South African woman jumped to the stage and led the crowd in a powerful call and response in the tradition of South African freedom fighters.

Amandla at a celebration at the New England Peace Pagoda,
Leverett, Massachusetts, 1989

Amandla rehearsal, Woolman Hill Conference Center, 1988

Typically, a strong-voiced leader yells "Amandla!" The crowd answers "Ngawethu!" to signify "The power is ours!" or "Power to the People!"

The young woman, a university student, said following the concert that she simply could not remain in her seat after hearing freedom songs from her homeland.

Just as my family's story originates from many sources, so too the Amandla Chorus came from many places and hearts. Like a freedom song, the chorus has no clear beginning or end. It builds on what came before, swimming in a swift stream of hope and defiance. Freedom songs flow under, over, and through forces that aim to keep people down, separated, and easy targets for domination. This powerful current sweeps singers along with determination and love.

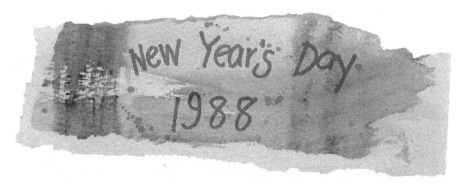

New Year's Day 1988

A recent transplant to Greenfield, Massachusetts, I hosted a meeting of the Pioneer Valley War Tax Resisters (PVWTR) on New Year's Day, 1988. At twenty-three, I had resisted paying United States income taxes for four years but hadn't spoken with others about my choice. A rag-tag, multi-generational bunch made up PVWTR: earnest, hardworking, and nearly all self-employed. Seasoned civil rights champions Wally and Juanita Nelson mentored the group.

We discussed peacemaking strategies, including refusing to support the US government in spending more than half of income-tax revenue on waging war.

Although we hoped to make a difference by refusing to fund what we opposed, most of us doubted our "effectiveness." We tried to live according to the principle "I don't do it to change the world; I do it so the world doesn't change me," wisdom attributed to several different twentieth-century activists.

Quietly singing "Siyahamba," I heated oil for popcorn during the meeting's break. Rosie Heidkamp from nearby Wendell asked, "How do you know that song?"

"From the collection *Freedom Is Coming*," I replied. "It's from South Africa."

"I know," said Rosie. "I spent part of my childhood there. We heard that song often as we walked past churches." Rosie's father sold Bibles door-to-door in South Africa, supporting a family of fourteen. Rosie asked, "Do you think you could teach that song, with all the harmonies, to me and a few friends?"

"Sure!" I answered. "I find Black South African hymns and freedom songs gorgeously rich in harmony and rhythm, but also very accessible."

"Let's get some people together," Rosie said with a grin. "Maybe we can use the Wendell Town Hall or the building across the street." I told her that if she secured a space, I'd put up flyers to see if more people might want to participate.

On a sunny, cold Sunday at the end of January, "a few friends" mushroomed to forty people. The session stretched to three hours as we sang freedom songs, filling the tiny former church with rousing harmonies. In the waning light, many people said they wouldn't leave unless I promised to hold another session. I promised.

Coming back East: Noonday Farm

Two weeks after my father's death, I headed west from New York State to spend the winter of 1985-1986 as a live-in volunteer at the Dorothy Day Hospitality House in Rochester, Minnesota. Drawn by the name of the woman who teamed up with Peter Maurin to initiate the Catholic Worker movement, I accepted the unpaid post in order to explore living in a community that embraced voluntary poverty and nonviolence. Another tenet of the Catholic Worker movement—offering hospitality to those without homes or hope—appealed to me.

In preparation, I added to my substantial collection of books and articles about Day, Maurin, and the history of the movement. Eagerly embarking on an adventure, I felt ready to devote myself to the task. But that Minnesota winter affected me far beyond severe wind chill factors as I attempted to negotiate living with and supporting people in distress. Close proximity to daily crisis was difficult enough; doing so surrounded by a wealthy, homogenous community—home of the Mayo Clinic as well as an enormous IBM campus—made the experience additionally confounding.

The Dorothy Day House was sponsored by a board of directors made up of Rochester residents who meant well yet seemed utterly unaware of what it means to live without such privileges as family connections, inherited money, skin color, and high-paying jobs. Some house rules struck me as unrealistic and cruel. For example, I felt unwilling to enforce the dictum

Eveline working on a roof at Noonday Farm,
Winchendon Springs, Massachusetts, 1986

that each guest must leave after two weeks' stay, regardless of
circumstances. I asked the board of directors if they believed
they would successfully turn their lives around in a fourteen-day
period if they faced homelessness, addiction, racism, and legacies
of abuse. Their responses demonstrated to me that we were
nowhere close to being on the same page.

Another rule, requiring guests to leave the house each day
between the hours of eight and five o'clock, seemed downright
dangerous, given the temperatures. I tried it myself for one
week, taking refuge during daylight hours in the public library
and other community spaces, but I found that the experiment
wore me down. After a few days, I felt utterly exhausted. I knew
the rules were put forth by people who intended to inculcate
self-reliance and ambition, yet I felt the expectations were not
only misguided but harmful.

After six months and numerous run-ins with the powers-that-be, I realized that I would never reconcile their version of hospitality with my understanding of the work and vision of Dorothy Day. Grateful for the experience, I decided to head back east. Though I had appreciated the change of scenery after years of watching my father decline and die, I wanted to reconnect with family and find a Catholic Worker community closer to home.

Noonday Farm in Winchendon Springs, Massachusetts, fit the bill. I loved the vibrant community immersed in reflection and humming with activism related to peace and justice. Noonday Farm comprised an intentional community of two families plus a few single people who came together with the avowed purpose of raising food for Boston soup kitchens and shelters while also pursuing social-justice work. Noonday folks welcomed me as a farm intern. I especially enjoyed performing with the Noonday Singers at rallies, protests, and worship services.

My two years at Noonday strongly influenced my later work with Amandla and Fiery Hope. I learned a lot about choral directing from Jim Levinson's energetic leadership and musical skills.

One Saturday, the adults spent the day in retreat at a New Hampshire monastery to discern our next steps in response to our government's covert actions in Central America. Songs punctuated our discussion.

We chose "Thuma Mina" as our post-lunch meditation song. Holding hands around a life-sized statue of Saint Francis of Assisi, we intended to sing for about ten minutes but continued for nearly an hour with a song that grew in meaning for me over many years.

Homegrown apartheid

We sang and spoke of South African apartheid during my first two years as Amandla's director. Our concerts felt deeply meaningful, and audience feedback encouraged us.

But something didn't feel right. We needed to look at injustice in our own country and communities. Even more difficult, we realized the importance of examining injustice in our own actions and attitudes.

We recognized deep connections between South African apartheid and institutional racism in the United States. We wanted to learn to name the subtle and overt ways people close to us — and millions we've never met — are oppressed every day. We learned about homegrown apartheid right here in the US.

By the time I was twenty-five, I knew what was next for Amandla. We needed to use the lessons we had learned — working and singing in the anti-apartheid movement — to turn our gaze on oppression under our noses.

Barwa

Paul Jones sang with Amandla in the early years, contributing great energy and ideas about how to connect with other musical and political organizers. Paul's creative thinking and boundless energy led Amandla to our wondrous association with Barwa, the singing group made up of South Africans studying and teaching in the Five Colleges, institutions of higher education of the Amherst-Northampton-South Hadley area. In fact, Paul's enthusiasm inspired Barwa members to form their group.

Paul sounded excited on the phone. "I met an amazing South African man at the Ladysmith show!" Paul went backstage after the show to meet members of the iconic singers of Ladysmith Black Mambazo, and to tell them about Amandla. An exuberant UMass faculty member stepped up with a grin.

"You sing South African freedom songs? I'm from South Africa!" The man shook Paul's hand. "I'm Mzamo Mangaliso. Hearing about your chorus makes me want to start a singing group of faculty and students. We have quite a number of South Africans at the Five Colleges, and you know they can sing!"

Paul passed Mzamo's phone number along to me.

Mzamo invited me to visit his family's Amherst home. Among the many gifts I received that day were Mzamo's time and patience in going over the various tones, clicks, stresses, and tongue placements of three gorgeous South African languages: Zulu, Sotho, and Xhosa. But the most beautiful gift of all was the way he opened his heart to a young, inexperienced choral director and budding political activist.

Mzamo is known for his warmth and generosity. Over many years he gave me joy and wisdom that extended to the Amandla Chorus and communities where we collaborated in performances throughout the northeastern US.

It didn't take Mzamo long to gather a group of fellow South Africans associated with the Five Colleges to form Barwa, which means "people of the bush." They were eager to share stories and songs with folks in the Pioneer Valley and beyond. We embarked on joint concerts and tours that gave Amandla singers an astonishing education.

We started small in December of 1988 with a performance at the Full Moon Coffeehouse in Wendell. We performed at Vermont's Putney School, a private high school, where our

Dr. Mzamo Mangaliso, founder and director of Barwa, directs the combined choirs
Barwa, Amandla, and the Noonday Singers
Providence, Rhode Island, June 1989.

concert had students leaping to their feet. If we had performed there on our own, Amandla would have lit a spark, but Barwa's energy and stories set that school community on fire.

June of 1989 brought a whirlwind of collaborative engagements. We participated in a series of large-scale events in Providence, Rhode Island, and Washington, DC. The events, attended by thousands, were orchestrated to raise awareness about anti-apartheid work and featured Allan Boesak, outspoken critic of the South African regime, and president of the World Alliance of Reformed Churches. Traveling and performing in major cities with Barwa brought new songs, ideas, and realizations to Amandla members.

The tour took place during Soweto Days, which commemorate the Soweto Uprising, a series of demonstrations and protests led by schoolchildren on the morning of June 16, 1976. While those courageous children took to the streets, I lived a peaceful, protected life at age twelve in upstate New York and southern Québec. I'd never heard of apartheid when my South African peers spoke up for justice in their land and were mowed down by police.

Thirteen years later—as we traveled by bus along the US eastern seaboard during a Soweto Days tour—an image burned in my brain. I couldn't shake the famous photo by Sam Nzima that became emblematic of the apartheid regime's viciousness: Hector Pieterson carried by Mbuyisa Makhubo after South African police shot him. His sister Antoinette runs beside them. Pieterson was rushed to a local clinic and pronounced dead on arrival.

How can grown men pump bullets into children? The question plagued me as our bus rolled south. Our tour helped me recognize more clearly that racism represents a terrible toxin in our human family, one we must address with education, compassion, the arts, and justice.

Upon returning home, Amandla and Barwa continued to work together and embraced a new collaboration with the phenomenal singer Jane Sapp. We did high-octane shows at UMass, the Academy at Charlemont, and the Shea Theater. It took hours for me to unwind after each show as I reverberated with explosive songs and passionate messages. Bringing our messages of justice to anyone who would listen, we also did quieter presentations in houses of worship and community centers.

We had no way of knowing that our partnership would take us into the presence of Nelson Mandela and Archbishop Desmond Tutu, allowing us to bring powerful songs to huge crowds. Nor could we have guessed that our team would travel to New York's largest maximum-security prison for one of the most hair-raising experiences of my life.

Following Mandela's release from nearly three decades in prison, things changed rapidly in South Africa. Many Barwa singers returned to their homeland to take up positions of leadership. For those who remained, workloads increased. The ranks of Barwa shrank as vital projects required their energy.

Years later, Mzamo reflected on that time: "What was so striking about you and the Amandla singers was your willingness to *learn* about other cultures through music. Note that I've emphasized the word 'learn.' To those of us who had recently arrived in the US, it was refreshing. The stereotypical American claims to be an expert in everything he/she does. You shattered that stereotype!"

co-op culture

When I moved to the Pioneer Valley in 1987, I worked part-time on a number of construction crews. I learned to grade and prepare sites, construct foundations, and keep an eye on the temperature in advance of pouring concrete. I built headers and knee walls, framed buildings, installed windows and doors, and put on siding. I didn't get into plumbing or wiring but often engaged in my personal favorite: roofing.

I grew up in an era when boys received tools, sports equipment, and toy vehicles as gifts while girls often got art supplies, dolls, and books. I loved those things and still do. But I also learned to love my tool belt and the feel of a good circular saw.

My brothers joined athletic teams and had options for scouting, while parents in our hometown generally steered girls toward skating and ballet. I loved those activities but felt grateful in my thirties when my brother Robert showed me how to work on my old Toyota.

During my twenties, some of my peers earned postgraduate degrees and settled into solid career tracks. I wanted the opposite: to experience as many types of employment as possible.

One of my favorite jobs, working at the Franklin Community Co-op in Greenfield, led to lifelong friendships. A few years after I stopped working at the tiny, funky storefront on Chapman Street, the co-op evolved into two stores: Green Fields Market on Greenfield's Main Street and McCusker's Market in beautiful Shelburne Falls.

No stranger to co-ops, I settled right in. My mother helped found the North Country Food Co-op in Plattsburgh shortly after I turned twelve. My brothers and I weren't always excited to find our plates covered by tofu and tempeh, sturdy brown rice, and hearty greens. Yet, as I grew older, I joined food co-ops no matter where I lived.

Being part of the co-op staff educated me about organic farming, community economics, and nutrition. My four-year stint as cashier and general grunt worker led to the satisfaction that comes with owning a business with a large group of wildly wonderful community members. I recall those early days with great fondness.

A co-op board member asked me to be staff liaison to the co-op board of directors. I attended a meeting at the home of board members Monica and Bob. I'd never been to a board meeting and expected formalities, but we all sat on the floor.

I knew Bob and Monica's kids, Jonah and Eila, from day care. In fact, earlier that day, three-year-old Jonah had faced down an infamous bully on the playground in defense of his two-year-old sister.

"Owen, you rat," he said, staring down a larger three-year-old. "You mess with my sister, you mess with me."

I noted that co-op members raised intrepid kids. I liked those people.

In attending co-op meetings, I observed Terry's expressiveness, Paul's thoughtfulness, Suzy's hilarity, and Steve's level-headedness.

Being a cashier introduced me to many people, a distinct advantage when I wanted to distribute material like copies of an eye-catching poster designed by local artist Marilyn Andrews for an Amandla event.

One of my co-op colleagues, Suzy Polucci, struck me as the funniest person alive and became a close friend. My life took a fascinating turn after Suzy invited me to join Blue Angel Arts, a theater company she worked with.

Things got heated at a co-op staff meeting. Some of the cashiers, resentful about the amount of work involved with opening and closing the store, protested having to move all of the produce into the walk-in cooler at night, and then back out for display in the morning.

Everyone knew the meeting would be emotional. Fortunately, Cheryl Fox, a trained mediator, facilitated the meeting, which otherwise would've fallen apart when two of the cashiers started crying and Karl jumped up on his chair and began yelling about the rights of workers. At one point, he used the word "proletariat," a word I'd encountered in books, but never in real life.

For some unknown reason, Patti, one of the co-managers, relayed a story from when she was in high school in New Jersey. Patti and a friend stripped off their clothes and streaked across the football field during a homecoming game in order to protest something—she didn't say what. Cheryl steered the meeting back on track, to the relief of the other co-manager, Janice. The meeting continued without any more crying or outbursts, and no one stripped off their clothes.

When I moved back east from my stint in Minnesota, I figured I would find similarly taciturn citizens in Franklin County. I'd heard that both Midwesterners and Yankees are famously reserved. Yet these folks reminded me more of my family in Québec—hand gestures, arm waving, shouting, raucous laughter.

I attended a co-op finance committee meeting and found it hard to believe the business would survive. It's not like people weren't trying. The committee charged Suzy with approaching a few wealthy members to ask for support, as she had a reputation for success in that department.

A couple of years earlier, Suzy had secured ten thousand dollars that kept the business solvent. But at the meeting I attended, she expressed doubts about her efficacy, claiming she'd bungled her previous assignment. She had approached a member whose great-aunt owned significant interest in a major television network. Hoping to tap deep pockets, Suzy arranged a meeting to ask for a gift.

When Suzy politely asked the great-niece of the wealthy TV magnate for money, the woman replied, "I need to consult my inner guide."

In her enthusiasm, Suzy misinterpreted the phrase "inner guide," instead hearing "Aunt Ida." Suzy replied, "Listen, we desperately need this gift to keep the co-op afloat. I'd be happy to travel to New York with you, and we could speak to your aunt together."

The co-op member said, "What the hell are you talking about?"

Suzy repeated her proposal, this time invoking the name "Aunt Ida." When this failed to clear up the confusion, Suzy asked, "Didn't you say you need to consult your Aunt Ida?"

The woman replied icily, "I did not say Aunt Ida. I need to consult my inner guide."

Suzy paused for a moment, and then said, "So we're not going to New York?"

The question further irritated the woman. Suzy then squarely hit the flusher: "Would it help if I had a talk with your inner guide?"

She probably should've quit sooner, but Suzy gave her all for the co-op.

Some co-op shifts were wacky beyond belief. One day, with thirty minutes left on my shift, I looked out the big front window and saw a notorious customer park her Volvo station wagon in front of the store. Luckily, this gave me time to brace myself. The scowling woman headed toward the door.

Entering the store, she said in a loud, angry tone, "I certainly hope my bulk order is finally in!"

I replied courteously, "I believe it arrived this morning" and directed her to the back room where people picked up orders.

She returned within fifteen seconds. "I can't find it anywhere," she moaned.

Setting aside the case of canned pinto beans I'd been pricing, I told a big fat lie: "I'd be happy to help you find it."

We headed up creaky stairs to the back room where a tower of boxes and mounds of bags awaited pick-up. I found orders for Jeanie and Joan and George and Ava, but none for this cheery customer. Finally, from the very bottom of the pile, I extracted her order.

She commented in a dreary tone, "Of course, it would be at the bottom." She read the label on the box. Shrieking, she exclaimed, "This contains non-fat dry milk powder! I can't eat this!" I had witnessed this woman throwing hissy fits before, but this one took the cake. One might think she'd found rat poison on the list of ingredients.

"You don't like non-fat dry milk powder?" I ventured timidly.

"It is not a pure food," she hissed. "I will not pay for this."

I heard the front door open and said, "I'm sorry, but I have to get back to the register. Janice will be back from the bank in about fifteen minutes. Maybe she can help you."

"I don't have fifteen minutes," snapped the woman. Referring to a nearby meditation center, she added, "I have to get up to Vipassana."

"Darn," I said. "Well, if you leave your phone number, I'll have Janice call you later."

"My phone number's on my bulk slip," she seethed.

"Alrighty, then," I replied. "Have a good rest of the day!"

I felt relieved that the next customers were friendly and non-combative: Joan and her three children, Alice, Julian, and Nora. Perhaps the co-op gods decided to make up for the recent exorcism in the back room.

I loved little Nora, whom I knew from the day care center. While Joan collected her bulk order from the back, her kids hung out, calm as can be.

Wearing blue sneakers and a long yellow T-shirt, Nora toddled over to a shelf, reaching for a box of arrowroot animal crackers. As she lifted her arms, her shirt hiked up, revealing the fact that she wore no pants. I glanced toward the back room, hoping Joan might reappear.

Although I knew Nora from daycare, I couldn't remember whether she belonged to the leaky crowd or whether she had the potty scene under control.

I walked to the front door and re-read the sign: "No shirt, no shoes, no service." No reference to pants.

With fifteen minutes left on my shift, I fervently prayed: *Dear, sweet Jesus, please prevent this child from pissing on the floor during the last moments of my shift. I will repent every irreverent thing I said or did in Catholic school. What I ask now, dear Lord, is for this child to hold her pee at least until Marshall arrives to take over. After that, Nora can let it rip. But if I have to clean up toddler juice, it will send me over the edge and you may as well bury me beneath a pile of non-fat dry milk powder.*

Just then, Marshall arrived. "I'm early," he said "I hitchhiked from Woolman Hill and got a ride right away. I can clock in now if you want."

"Are you sure?" I asked innocently. "Well, it's been a busy shift, so I'll take you up on your offer. Have fun!"

I hung up my apron and sprinted out the door.

After a few years at the co-op, I felt the job-change bug bite me again, and moved on to work at the collectively owned Green River Café a few streets over. I came on board as entertainment manager and became a part owner in a fast-paced, hilarious, and largely dysfunctional restaurant. (Since then, I've heard from many sources that nearly all restaurants are dysfunctional, but I've not tested the theory.)

At the Café, I also waited on tables and did a few shifts of cooking and washing dishes. I learned new skills as a sound engineer. I stayed a few years, and then moved on.

I've loved all of my jobs. When I moved to Franklin County in 1987, I planned to stay in the area a year or two, but I chose to settle here because of the wonderful people who populate my stories.

The co-op culture I found in Franklin County echoed a culture I recognized from another of my home places in nearby Québec. In St. Germain de Grantham and Drummondville, there are cooperative bookstores, auto mechanics, housecleaning co-ops, and banks. When we bury family members, we do so through le Donais Coopérative Funéraire.

Not surprisingly, the co-op and Amandla, sometimes interwove throughout the years. The chorus has been invited to sing at the co-op on Martin Luther King Days, and the co-op board sometimes looks similar to an Amandla small group ensemble.

Every time I walk into a co-op, it feels like home. Due to the high volume of friends and acquaintances and the ensuing conversations, it sometimes takes ninety minutes to purchase a head of broccoli and a block of cheese. But what a wonderful way to shop and to live.

singing for Señor Chávez

An Amandla singer and union organizer invited the chorus to sing at a July, 1989 rally in Springfield that would feature a speech by César Chávez.

I imagined us singing to a great swell of humanity, union supporters drawn to hear Chávez, the iconic Mexican-American labor leader and civil rights activist who, with Dolores Huerta, co-founded the National Farm Workers' Association in the early sixties, later to be known as the United Farm Workers or UFW.

Chávez's work inspired me during my teens, and I displayed a prized poster in each of my living spaces during my itinerant post-teen years. The poster was a Chávez quote, ending with:

> It's ironic that those who till the soil, cultivate and harvest the fruits, vegetables, and other foods that fill your tables with abundance have nothing left for themselves.

Preparing to sing at the rally, I pictured Señor Chávez still at the top of his game. I was unaware of difficulties in the inner workings of the UFW. I won't attempt to detail the issues here but instead will share a story of singing freedom songs under odd circumstances.

Arriving at the rally site, we found a barren parking lot with a few dozen people, a far cry from my pipe dream of a verdant park filled with hundreds of workers holding neatly lettered signs. *Probably just the staging area,* I thought. *We'll proceed to a grander site.* I turned to my union friend and said, "This must be where we warm up."

"Nope. This is it." He gestured to a flatbed truck parked near a portable toilet. "There's our stage."

He brought us to a trailer parked at the lot's edge. "We can warm up here." The singers seemed underwhelmed and I feared our energy could dissipate.

Trying to sound enthusiastic, I said to the dozen singers: "I want to teach you an easy song that's perfect for today!"

They fixed me in a collective gaze reserved for impromptu Amandla moments: *You want us to do WHAT? All right, if you say so . . .*

They're such good sports.

I taught parts to "We Shall Not Give Up the Fight" from a collection of South African freedom songs. The singers learned it within minutes.

> We shall not give up the fight, we have only started
> we have only started, we have only started . . .

Spirits rose as we learned the other verses:

> Together we'll have victory, hand holding hand,
> hand holding hand, hand holding hand . . .
> Never ever put to flight, we are bound to win,
> we are bound to win, we are bound to win . . .

By the time organizers fetched us for the rally, we no longer cared whether the gathering involved ten or ten thousand people. We felt ready for anything.

Well, almost anything. The wind picked up by the time we assembled on our flat-bed stage to huddle around mics. Singers held each mic stand firmly to prevent the gale from flinging them from the flatbed.

Surely someone will call this off?

An organizer gave me a desperate hand sign. We began "Freedom Is Coming" while clutching mic stands and each other. After two songs, I felt parched and realized I'd forgotten my water bottle. I applied lip balm to help with dryness but wiped it off after my lips became instantly coated with grit. The wind flung particles in every direction.

We prepared to sing our last song, the new one, and the wind died down like someone had hit a switch. We sang the opening chord from the calm flatbed and the singers rediscovered our joy in this spirited song.

I glanced at Chávez. Cupping an ear, he moved closer to the stage. He nodded and beamed, so we repeated the song several times. Dusty rally attendees picked up the song, and the gritty parking lot was transformed to . . . a gritty parking lot with a straggly group of folks filled with the joy of singing a powerful song.

As we descended the steps, Señor Chávez came to the stage for his speech. He said, "That's a very good song! I would like to talk with you afterwards."

His words were inspiring, but he was clearly fatigued from years of struggle. I had no way of knowing that this principled man, though only in his sixties, would live fewer than four more years.

After his speech, he came down the steps without taking his eyes off the singers. "How do you find such songs?" he asked. "How long have you sung together?"

We discussed freedom songs and remaining committed to long-term struggles for justice. When we parted, he repeated emphatically, "That last one is a very good song. I hope you keep singing."

On the trip home, I thought, *The dust we endured for a few minutes was nothing compared to conditions farmworkers of all ages endure all day, every day.*

Despite the rally's small turnout and hardscrabble venue, I knew the day was a success because we'd met a great soul and left feeling enriched and inspired.

Relief

The auditorium at the University of Massachusetts, Amherst, was stifling in one-hundred-degree heat. One Amandla singer, eight months pregnant, looked like she might faint. I kept it together by thinking about the stream of cold water I'd soon stand under at home.

Maybe they don't have air-conditioning. Or it's broken.

Two more songs, and we're done.

Moments after we came offstage, though, I delayed my hasty exit when an audience member said she wished to speak with me privately. The urgency in her voice convinced me to find a quiet spot.

She told me a neighbor had sexually violated her in the 1950s when she was nine. Haltingly and then in a torrent of words, she related how the abuse occurred for three years. She told her parents and later a teacher, but no one believed an influential member of the community would do such a thing.

"They said I lied. One day, my mother caught him in the act," she shrugged. "She blamed me for enticing him."

The physical abuse ended, but she continued to feel blamed. Her assailant moved away.

Despite the heat, I felt cold while listening to the woman's story.

"But here's what I really want to say," she continued. "When you sang 'Circle Round for Freedom,' I felt tears welling up."

Linda Hirschhorn's song touches many audience members, but this woman's comments conveyed urgent gratitude.

"I feel numb most of the time. I'm rarely able to cry. But tonight, the tears . . . I cried! Tears came down my cheeks." She looked radiant.

She described productive healing work she'd done as an adult. Yet actual crying eluded her.

"When tears come," she said, "I feel wholeness and grace. In those moments, I believe I can truly heal."

I wanted to envelop her in a hug but felt uncertain about boundaries with someone who'd suffered such horrible transgressions in childhood.

She took my hand and said, "What a gift. Thank you."

At home under a cool shower, I felt how water droplets can take the edge off punishing heat that, moments earlier, seemed inescapable.

Tall, Handsome, and sings like God

A staff member at the western Massachusetts coeducational private school showed us to the auditorium and said, "The students will be here in half an hour. This is an All-School. Bathrooms are that way." He left and we did vocal warmups before the entire student body arrived.

It was the week before Martin Luther King Day, 1994. We'd been invited to celebrate diversity; I knew this could mean very different things, depending on the institution. I'd seen enough to know that, in many places, it was about checking off a box in order to seem polite. Once the program was done, though, it was back to business as usual.

I wonder how it is at this school? Given what I'd seen — crisp, stylish buildings, athletic fields, the pond — it was tempting to draw conclusions. But I didn't want to presume. *Give them a chance,* I thought.

I reflected on my drafty firetrap of a high school. *Nothing like this!* I ran the singers through a few songs.

"Dennis? You up for the solo?" The tall, handsome fellow grinned. I knew he would nail the lead to "Gabi, Gabi." A tenor who sang in the Dutch Reformed Church as a child, Dennis aced the solo every time. *He'll blow their socks off,* I thought, gleefully. *Wait 'til they hear him sing like God!*

The students filed in. I noticed the first couple of rows were quickly filled by what we'd called jocks at my high school.

Dennis Helmus at the Sirius Community, Shutesbury, Massachusetts where Amandla sang at an "Interdependence Day" event July 4, 1992

Elbowing, high-fiving, goofing around, they joked with one another.

The concert began with a mix of African, African-American, and Central American songs. There was polite applause after each song and a few nods as we shared justice-themed quotes and poems.

The jocks seemed amused but remained generally respectful.

When Dennis stepped up to the microphone, I blew the pitch pipe and stood back to let him work his magic. His voice landed on the opening note with strength and clarity. Dennis sang with his eyes closed, head tipped back slightly. The chorus responded to his clarion phrases first in Zulu, then in English. We sang of captives freed and bread given to the hungry.

I became aware of noisy activity in the front rows. Facing the choir and pantomiming *Smile!* I avoided what I customarily do in concert: turning around, connecting, encouraging the audience. I felt tension rise as sounds coming from just behind me increased in volume. We were headed for trouble.

A situation ensued that, if given a chance, I'd handle so differently today.

The song ended, and someone attempted a parody of Dennis doing the lead, making it sound absurd and frilly. "Do that again, sissy," came a voice in a low, menacing tone. My eyes darted to Dennis to see if he'd heard.

He'd heard. His head held high, the picture of dignity, he took deep, deliberate breaths.

Mean-spirited laughter punctuated a rumble of voices, leading to the pièce de résistance. A sharp voice rang out: "FAGGOT!"

Silence followed the slur. I knew everyone had heard. I scanned the auditorium. Some students looked at their laps; a few smirked. There was no sound.

No faculty member marched to the front. No administrator interrupted to put things right.

Nothing. Happened.

Then, slowly, came laughter. Rolling, pointed laughter. The jocks in the front rows erupted while the rest of us simply looked on. No one else moved a muscle. The jocks enjoyed their fun while the rest of us did absolutely nothing.

I felt that the people who ran the school betrayed and deserted us. Clearly, I was on my own in dealing with the misguided schoolboys. I've suffered a lifelong curse in response to difficult situations: I grow terribly hot in the face. I knew my cheeks were crimson.

Dammit! I thought. *What do I do?* I hated those boys more than all the bullies I'd ever known, combined. Rage flashed through me and I wondered, not for the first time, *Where are the adults? Why do they let this crap happen?*

The peanut gallery continued to gloat. I was on the verge of tears but had no intention of giving them the satisfaction of seeing me cry.

Glancing at the exits, the singers whispered uneasily to each other. I hadn't yet learned that my role as choral director enables me to challenge disruptive audience members. I reached for what I considered my only tool: a song. Locking eyes with Dennis, I lifted my pitch pipe in a gesture of helplessness and shrugged as if to say, Should we keep going?

He nodded.

I'll never come here again, I vowed. *In the meantime, we'll sing.*

We sang and delivered quotes and poems over the jerks' heads. *They're not here,* I pretended. *They don't deserve to be here. Screw them. We're doing a concert. Celebrate diversity, indeed.*

We finished the surreal event to a moment or two of polite applause. Then the audience vanished. How can so many people vacate an auditorium at once? Not a single student remained. Faculty and administrators were nowhere in sight. *Did I dream it?* I wondered. *Were people really even here?*

We hurried to our cars. We huddled around Dennis in the parking lot and shared choice words about the morons in the front rows and the negligent staff. "How can that happen," I railed, "with no response from those in charge?"

"Oh, trust me," Dennis said, rolling his eyes. He let us know that this was far from being the first time such a thing had happened to him.

I admitted to feeling like a failure. One singer said, "We're all responsible. But we were totally unprepared for the attack."

Another singer chimed in, "I've worked in schools. I can't believe we were left to our own devices to deal with their kids!"

I explained that I'd been sure a staff member would intervene; my brain had frozen. Of course, after the fact, I came up with dozens of things I could have said or done. "I blew it."

One friend said, "Don't beat yourself up." She suggested I call the school. Dennis nodded.

When I arrived home, I dumped my bag in the foyer and picked up the phone, asking to speak with the head of school. He was unavailable. Identifying myself once more, I said it was important. He was busy.

I called again the next day, saying that if the head of school could not come to the phone, I would visit in person and wait until he could find a moment to speak with me.

He came on the line and said, "Yes?" He sounded annoyed. I registered my dismay at his students' behavior and said I was disappointed in the lack of intervention by faculty or administration.

His response floored me.

"Well, you know how it is," he said, referring to the bullies as members of a sports team. "They mean no harm," he said, revealing fondness and admiration. "They're high spirited."

"That's what you call public taunting and homophobia?" I sputtered. "High spirited?!"

"Now, now," he said. "Let's avoid hysteria. They're just kids."

My next stream of words probably struck him as a rant. I insisted that precisely because they were kids, they needed guidance to develop into respectful individuals. I did not employ tools of cool persuasion. I laid it on pretty thick, most likely to try to make up for my previous day's helplessness.

"They are good boys," he countered stiffly. "Are you telling me how to run my school?" Both angry, we got nowhere.

Regaining his cool, smooth voice, he concluded, "You and I hold a diversity of opinions. Thank you for coming to our school. Good luck to you." With that, he hung up.

There's that word diversity again, I thought. *So handy to throw around.*

If I could choose a life mistake to re-do, that scenario would be a top contender.

Hate Crime

Amandla singers filled the steps of Northampton City Hall in June of 1998 and sang to the crowd in support of two men who'd been badly beaten by a carload of young men from Chicopee who'd come to town with the intention of "pounding some faggots."

We heard speeches, joined chants, and shouted our resolve until we were hoarse. Yet I left with a sinking feeling.

One of the men assaulted by heavy work boots as he lay writhing on the sidewalk was Dennis, the Amandla tenor who sang the lead to "Gabi, Gabi." His partner, a concert pianist, sustained injuries that affected his playing for a long time.

We have a lot of work to do.

singing for elders

Residents of the Longmeadow assisted living community arrived for our 2007 show. Witnessing our warm-up vocalizations, they hesitated at the door but we smiled and gestured that they should come on in.

Several people arrived in wheelchairs. Some came with canes or walkers. A few moved with confidence. The audience nearly filled the large, lovely space. The crowd represented an age span of three decades or more, bringing to mind my first experiences with older folks in an institutional setting.

When we were eleven years old in 1975, my best friend Cassie and I watched with interest as a multi-story building went up near my house. The largest building in my residential neighborhood, it was the only one not a single-family home or duplex.

When the facility opened and we saw people coming and going, Cass and I approached the automatic door, marveling at glass and shiny metal.

Busy with clipboards and a telephone, a woman about my mom's age sat at a large desk in the pristine lobby. We stood waiting before her until she hung up the phone and smiled, exuding efficiency and brisk friendliness. "Who are you here to visit? Just sign your names here and put the room number."

"I, um, well, we're just . . ." I fumbled.

Ever eloquent and focused, Cass stepped in. "We don't actually know anyone who lives here, but we'd like to ask about volunteering."

The receptionist set down her pen. "Oh! We don't have a volunteer program yet." She shuffled papers and rearranged pens in a cup. "Please wait a moment. I'll call the activities director."

Pushing two buttons and turning away from us slightly, she addressed someone in a voice laced with amusement. She tried to shield her words by covering the mouthpiece with one hand, but we heard her say, "SO cute! I know! Can you come down?" Cass and I rolled our eyes.

Cass Hartnett, left, Eveline's best friend since sixth grade, with Eveline in 1992

Despite the cool, institutional air, I began to sweat. Knowing we weren't being taken very seriously, I felt awkward. At eleven, I felt awkward much of the time.

Elevator doors opened and a woman holding a clipboard walked toward us purposefully.

I noted that clipboards were a hot item in this place and wondered if I should borrow one from my dad.

Wearing a crisp lime-green skirt and jacket ensemble and glasses with smart black frames, the activities director said hello and asked if she could help us. She wore an awful lot of lipstick, and her every movement set off clouds of perfume.

Cassie explained our plan; I nodded. The lime-green woman put a pen between her teeth and tapped her foot while looking around the lobby. She blinked rapidly. The other woman, still seated behind the desk, looked amused.

Suddenly Lime-Green interrupted Cass and said, brightly, "I know! You can help with bowling! When the residents knock the pins down, you can set them back up!" She blinked, grinning widely as though inviting us to participate in a grand adventure. Cass and I tried not to sigh.

Diplomatically, Cass replied, "Sure," drawing the syllable out slowly. "We could do that." Leaning in toward the woman, she confided, "Actually, we were hoping for something a little more one-on-one, or in our case, two-on-two. Ev and I have great people skills."

The women nodded at Cass and glanced dubiously at me.

The seated receptionist cupped her hand near her mouth and whispered loudly, "Eleanor and Jane."

Lime-Green snapped her fingers and said, "Wait a minute! We have two residents who don't receive visitors. They share a room." She unclipped papers from her clipboard and immediately reclipped them, having lined up all the bottoms and sides just so.

"I suppose I could set you up as volunteer visitors after a brief intake. Do your parents know you're here? Can I have their phone numbers? Maybe you could visit the ladies for a half-hour or so." With that, we were swept into the main office.

Thanks to Cassie's confidence and clear head, we were able to form deep bonds with two dear women. Our commitment lasted until we left middle school and our lives became too busy.

I learned what a mistake it is to look at a roomful of elders and assume "they're just a bunch of old folks." I had made that assumption prior to my visits to Meadowbrook Nursing Home.

The last time I visited my hometown, I saw the name had been upgraded to "Meadowbrook Healthcare / Skilled Nursing and Rehabilitation." But it looked like the same place, plus forty years of wear.

The hours Cass and I spent visiting with Eleanor and Jane showed me that each elder overflows with memories full of joy, sadness, wisdom, and loss. Elders' stories are funny, surprising, and riveting.

After singing "This Little Light of Mine," "Over the Rainbow," and a few non-English songs, I looked out over the sweet, appreciative audience in Longmeadow and asked, "Has anyone here ever been a teacher?" A couple of hands went up, uncertainly.

I heard someone say, "What did she say?"

I moved closer to the microphone and asked again.

Several more hands went up.

Staying close to the mic, I asked a series of questions: Has anyone worked in medicine? Manufacturing? Engineering? How many have raised children? Lived on a farm? Born in a country outside the US?

The residents seemed shy at first. Soon, however, hands shot up and folks looked around to see how others responded. I heard exclamations of surprise and, within minutes, the room was abuzz.

With the room in a light uproar, I asked a final question: Was anyone here overseas during WWII or have a loved one overseas? The room fell silent. Several hands went up slowly, then more hands. A woman in the second row patted the arm of the woman sitting to her left. Heads bowed.

"I'm continually amazed," I said, "that each human being is a treasure trove of stories and wisdom. It's so wonderful to be here with you today. We look forward to chatting with you at the end of the show."

In the spring of 2017, we presented an upbeat performance and sing-along in the dining hall of an assisted living facility in Greenfield. Finishing up, we headed toward the lobby. Singers' faces glowed as they noted how fun it is when folks sing along and really get into it.

I paused at the main desk and asked, "If I could get some singers to stay a little while longer, could we offer a few songs in the Reflections Unit?" That's what they call the locked section for folks with Alzheimer's and other forms of dementia.

The receptionist shrugged. I added, "I should've thought of it sooner. Maybe it's too last-minute?"

"Let me check!" she said good-naturedly. "I'm sure they'd love it. I just need to see if they're in the middle of something."

A brief call indicated that we were welcome to go upstairs. I turned to ask for volunteers and found the singers right with me, having followed the exchange. Nearly all said, "I'll do it!" Two expressed regret that they couldn't stay due to other obligations.

We took the stairs to the second floor. Something about stairways makes our chorus extra boisterous; banter echoed off the walls. As we approached the second floor, I said, "Sh-sh-shhhhh!" It became a giant game of telephone as they wildly shushed each other. *They're boisterous even when trying to be quiet,* I thought fondly.

We entered the secure area and found eight women sitting on couches. They spent most of each day in that big room eating meals, making crafts, watching movies, and receiving visitors. The space seemed light and airy. I knew the Reflections Unit residents regularly took walks with staff members around the circular first floor loop and into the gorgeous courtyard. I could tell the staff was kind. Yet my heart ached for lost cognition and freedom, and I'm aware of the nagging question: *Will it happen to me?*

We greeted the staff and the ladies. Some looked delighted while others looked vacant. We sang upbeat songs as some women clapped along. One woman, who seemed very present and capable, called out requests, and we tried to oblige. We didn't know enough of the words to pull off the songs, but she helped us through. In the song lyric department, she proved sharp as a tack.

After fifteen minutes, a staff member glanced at her watch, and I asked, "Should we wrap it up?"

She signaled that we could do one more. "They love it," she said, smiling. "But yes. We need to wrap up soon."

"Ladies, we're going to do a familiar song. See if you can guess which movie it's from." Just a few notes into Peter Amidon's arrangement of "Over the Rainbow" came cries of "WIZARD OF OZ!! I LOVE THAT MOVIE!"

Through it all, though, one woman sat unmoving. No expression showed on her face; I couldn't even detect evidence of respiration. She blinked once or twice, but other than that, she may as well have been a statue. Her stylishly coifed hair and finely constructed face gave her a regal air accentuated by her long, graceful nose, perfectly formed eyebrows, and high cheekbones. She looked stately and absent.

I noticed space next to her on the couch, so I sat while motioning to the singers to repeat "Over the Rainbow." I took the woman's hand. At the feeling of skin on skin, she turned toward me urgently as if on the verge of revealing a long-kept secret. Her body language became alive and insistent as she leaned toward me, opening her mouth.

Closing her mouth, she shook her head. I squeezed her hand and leaned closer to sing softly in her ear, "Where troubles melt like lemon drops away above the chimney tops, that's where you'll find me . . . "

Again, her face conveyed great energy and insistence. Her mouth worked as though forming words, but no sound came out.

Tears ran down her cheeks. Her expression remained impassive as tears poured out of her.

When the song ended, she took one of my hands in both of hers and said with striking clarity, "I don't know why I'm crying." She broke into an enormous smile. "I'm crying . . . I can't remember why . . . what is it? I don't know. It feels WONDERFUL!" A staff member hovered nearby, astonished. The beautiful elder repeated, "I'm crying. It feels wonderful."

That's where you'll find me . . .

Joy to the world

Fifteen singers met in Shelburne on Christmas morning, 1996, to share a mix of holiday music and freedom songs with residents of a quaint, rambling rest home. We'd sung there the month before, and on the way out that day, I had asked the social director, "When do you most need singing here?"

"Christmas morning!" she said.

"OK," I said, figuring I could get a few Amandla members to join me. "We'll come Christmas morning!"

Her eyes grew large. "I was kidding . . . I mean, I didn't think you'd actually say yes." She added, "Holiday mornings are the hardest times to cheer the residents. We do everything we can to make it festive, but it's tough for those who stay here instead of going home with family."

"What time would you like us here Christmas morning?" I asked.

"You'll really come? Wow. OK. How about ten o'clock?" She hugged me.

On Christmas morning, some residents clapped or sang along in the day room while others looked drowsy or vacant. One man looked asleep or comatose. Strapped to a reclining chair, he didn't open his eyes unless a kindly attendant prodded him. His helper, a middle-aged woman with thick glasses, gently nudged him every few minutes. She pointed to us, but each time, the man closed his eyes again and re-inhabited his stupor, mouth hanging open, stubbly chin on his chest.

As the presentation drew to a close, I asked one singer named Koco if he'd share a Christmas song from his native Guatemala. Koco grinned, shyly. A moment later, he stepped forward, pulling a harmonica from among several in a pouch on his belt.

Koco played a jaunty version of "Joy to the World," foot tapping, head bobbing. I glanced at the strapped-in fellow. His eyes were open and his mouth was closed. Slowly, a smile formed, blossoming into a full-fledged grin. His face transformed as his eyes shone.

Koco finished the song, and a hearty cheer went up. The man who, moments earlier, seemed so far away attempted to clap with hands that looked stiff. His attendant helped him to bring his hands together in awkward applause, which only broadened his grin. Several times, the attendant brought her shoulder to her face in quick jabs, and I saw she stemmed a flow of tears.

Afterwards, she approached the singers. "I've been here six years. Never saw him smile before!"

the prisoner, the astronaut, and the drop-out

I surveyed my costume collection on the day before Halloween, 1998. Kids at the after-school program where I worked had asked with great excitement if I would join them in dressing up the next day. Of course I said yes.

My mummy costume, left over from a show I did with Suzy Polucci, appeals to kids of all ages. I laid the costume on the bed and remembered that I had changed it from mummy to sperm per Suzy's instruction for a different character in a subsequent performance. I suspected the mummy might go over better with the young set, so I adjusted the costume once again.

As I prepared for Halloween, I noticed that the front page of the newspaper featured a photo of Senator John Glenn in full astronaut gear. I felt envious, wishing I could get ahold of that costume. At age seventy-seven, Glenn prepared to return to outer space. The first American to orbit the earth, he circled it three times in 1962, a couple of years before my birth.

A phone call from a friend on Halloween Eve also brought news that the Pennsylvania Supreme Court had denied Mumia Abu-Jamal another trial, meaning the governor could sign his death warrant at any time.

I adjusted my mummy wraps while pondering ways in which John Glenn and Mumia Abu-Jamal had affected my life.

A year earlier, the poet Martín Espada and I met to discuss our collaborations for an event to benefit the Western Massachusetts Prison Issues Group (WMPIG). Martín suggested I write a choral piece to accompany his poem about Mumia Abu-Jamal. That poem, "Another Nameless Prostitute Says the Man Is Innocent," begins powerfully with lines that include the phrase ". . . knew what happened . . . " repeated throughout the first stanza.

I came up with a hypnotic chant. Basses and tenors trade off with altos and sopranos, singing one name over and over: "Mumia!" The Amandla singers performed it with Martín on October 29, 1997.

In an article for *The Progressive,* Martín describes Mumia as "an eloquent African-American journalist convicted in the 1981 slaying of police officer Daniel Faulkner in Philadelphia—under extremely dubious circumstances." Mumia sat on Pennsylvania's death row for many years, sent there by the notorious Judge Albert Sabo, who put more people on death row than any other sitting judge in the US. A twelve-member jury unanimously found Mumia guilty after three-hours' deliberation. In 2011, his death sentence was commuted to life imprisonment after Philadelphia District Attorney R. Seth Williams no longer pursued the death penalty.

Many people believe the notorious case is pervaded by cover-ups. The case seems emblematic of imbalances in our nation's judicial system.

I felt relieved in 1982 when graduation day finally arrived, and I left my Catholic high school. My classmates and I had moved cautiously for four long years under the disapproving eyes of Brothers of Christian Instruction and a few nuns in an ancient building with worn wooden floors. Our wardens distrusted our youth, our hormones, and any new ideas.

During my sophomore year in high school, the principal threatened to suspend me for refusing to say the pledge of allegiance. I explained that I would say the pledge "when there's liberty and justice for all in this country."

Unmoved, the principal called my mom and asked her to pick me up. After describing my transgression, the principal listened for a few moments as my mother offered comments I couldn't hear.

"Just come and get her," the principal said, slamming down the receiver.

Mom arrived at the principal's office looking angry. I figured I was in for it. When Mom spoke, however, I realized her anger was not directed at me. "You will not suspend my daughter for acting on her beliefs," she said firmly. Mom told me to wait in the hall.

The thought of my diminutive mother going head to head with the enormous nun made me smirk, but when the door re-opened, I put on a bland expression.

The principal sputtered, "Go back to class!"

Mom said, "I'll see you at home." Suppressing a smile, she swept past me.

Somehow, I made it through high school. My parents gave me a pocket calculator after the graduation ceremony. They also told me that my dad had advanced cancer. The news settled my college plans: Mom would need help, so I'd attend Plattsburgh State, the university in my hometown, where I would receive enough grants and scholarships to cover tuition.

At summer's end, most of my friends packed up and left for far-flung schools. I consoled myself with the thought that, having received permission to take more classes during my first semester than normally allowed freshmen, I'd be able to graduate in three years if I maintained that pace.

I thrived in environments of open discussion and debate. When the activist priest Daniel Berrigan spoke at Plattsburgh State, he asked the college president to arrange a meeting with some politically active students. Thrilled to be one of six chosen, I sat at Berrigan's feet and marveled at how different it was from high school. Professors like Daphne Kutzer, Carol Leonard, and Douglas Skopp encouraged me to think broadly and act decisively.

In my third semester, one of my professors said, "You're a great candidate for a Truman Scholarship." She handed me a brochure describing awards "designed to provide opportunities for outstanding students to prepare for careers in public service."

"All you have to do," she said, "is fill out the application and write an essay analyzing a public policy issue of your choice in six hundred words or less. A review committee in Princeton, New Jersey, will decide whether you're Truman material."

I knew Harry S Truman had dropped atomic bombs on the Japanese, so I had a hard time imagining myself a Truman scholar. But my professor insisted, "Fill out the application. It's a lot of money."

What the hell? I thought. *If I express my real opinions, the review committee will shred my application.*

My essay, "A Conflict of Interest: The Press and the Government," begins

> A credible press is vital for the function of any democratic system. There is, however, a conflict of interest calling into question whether a super-power state and a credible press may co-exist.

I received a letter notifying me that I was a finalist and that Senator John Glenn would travel to Plattsburgh to interview me.

I felt stunned and wanted to back-pedal.

The day of the interview, I arrived at a posh suite on the top floor of the administration building. I stared at the plush carpeting, built-in bar, and thick draperies. I hadn't realized such a room existed on our campus, where classrooms and lecture halls often seemed overheated or too cold and where many walls and ceilings were decorated with chipped or peeling paint.

I sat at a big, shiny table with several faculty members and administrators. No one spoke. Finally, the college president arrived, steering the senator by the elbow, looking chummy. Two of the senator's aides trailed behind. Everyone stood up quickly, so I did, too.

University reps fawned over Glenn. To me, he just looked bald and bored. He said hello to everyone, me last. Actually, he barely looked at me.

Senator Glenn leafed through my packet while others peppered me with questions. I felt hypocritical. I didn't want to be a Truman scholar. I didn't care about the money. I knew that, in addition to using incendiary nuclear devices, Truman refused to consider an appeal in the Rosenberg case and helped sow the seeds of the Vietnam War.

I wanted out. The posh suite made me claustrophobic, and I yearned to get away from the senator and the others who smelled of money, power, and indifference. I felt listless and gave dull, monosyllabic responses. One faculty member glared at me, unable to believe that the school's prize candidate had turned into a zombie.

The senator kept leafing through my packet. Suddenly, he interjected: "What's this?"

Uh-oh, I thought. *He found my essay.*

His face clouded over. He looked at me for the first time. "You don't think we have a free press?" he asked sharply.

I took a long breath and said, "No, Senator, I do not."

"We live in the most free nation in the world. What makes you think, young lady, that our press isn't objective?"

Everyone glared at me. I didn't care. I saw my way out: the truth. I knew that if I simply told the truth, it would spring me from that oppressive room. "Well, Senator, since both the government and the media are owned by large corporations, I think using the word 'objectivity' when referring to the mainstream press is a joke. Come to think of it, using the word 'democracy' in this country is probably a joke, as well."

For a few moments, I free-floated in outer space with Senator John Glenn, the famous astronaut. Then sound and air returned as Glenn slapped my application on the table and said, "Thank you for your time." He got up to leave.

Suddenly, everyone scurried about. No one looked at me.

I dropped out of college shortly after sabotaging the Truman scholarship. Dad grew sicker, and I had to find a real job.

I incurred no penalty for speaking my truth to Senator Glenn. I just said what I thought and left. They let me go. Apparently, a white, nineteen-year-old, low-income, female college student didn't strike them as a threat.

Mumia has been heavily penalized in ways most people can't even imagine.

Years after my ill-fated interview, I looked at Glenn's photo in the paper and marveled that American tax dollars can send a privileged white man to outer space while a dreadlocked visionary sat on death row.

I'll never forget how I felt after the senator left my essay on the table. When I think about John Glenn and Mumia Abu-Jamal, I know which one, for me, represents true freedom.

Working with gifted mentors shapes my work. Musicians, poets, writers, activists and other great souls show me ways to keep my balance in a culture that's not always kind to those who try to bring about justice by trafficking in the arts. As I honor mentors, Suzy Polucci's influence and gifts deserve special mention.

I wrote the following tribute during the summer of 2017 and sent it to Suzy in September. She replied, "I feel honored down to my bone marrow. I can't wait to read your book. Thank you for the many ways you love me and love our world."

Suzy began experiencing troubling physical symptoms a few weeks after our

Suzy Polucci, left, with Eveline at Laurel Lake in Erving, Massachusetts, 1995

The Thin Ice Theater Troupe wrote and performed political and cultural satire.
They are, clockwise from top, Rupert Clark (Spidey),
Joshua Jay "Waffles" Dostis (with fork and spoon), Eveline (fiddle),
Martin Church (in drag), Jack Golden (salesman in plaid), Paul Richmond (priest),
Joseph DiCenso (with keyboard), and Suzy, the pirate in the center.

exchange. In February of 2018, Suzy learned she had Creutzfeldt-Jakob disease, a rare (one in a million) degenerative brain disorder. Suzy died at home on March 27, 2018.

Gillis MacDougall, left, with Suzy, who brought him the costume he's wearing on his birthday

Changing my tribute to Suzy from the present to past tense proved one of the hardest tasks of my life. Suzy's absence leaves a hole wide and deep. Still, her brilliance continues to shine in countless ways.

I met Suzy in the late 1980s through working at the co-op, political theater, and community activism. She asked me to join her in presenting original productions, first in Blue Angel Arts and later in Thin Ice Theater. Both companies operated

Suzy, left, as the Grim Reaper at an October 31, 1997, protest in Greenfield of the death penalty; Eveline confronts then Lieutenant Governor Paul Celucci.

mainly out of Wendell. Under Suzy's direction, I witnessed an extraordinary model of collaborative artistic work.

Earlier in life, I performed with orchestras and other ensembles and met good, kind players. Yet, the classical music world seemed pervaded with competitive, chilly reserve. I grew up in that world, but it didn't feel like home.

Joining the Noonday Singers as a young adult was a revelation of warmth and deep personal regard. I blossomed while singing with a group of activists who walked their talk in lifestyle, work, and personal sacrifice.

Upon meeting Suzy, I noticed how she demonstrated care for her friends and colleagues. She proved that it's possible for artistic teamwork to be mutually supportive and emotionally rich. Yet her compassion did not slow her down. A creative cyclone, she turned out brilliant work, but her cyclone enhanced creativity and friendships rather than destroying everything in its path.

She was the funniest person I'd ever met as well as a skilled actor, educator, writer, artistic innovator, director, comic, mediator, and advocate for those who've experienced trauma.

Suzy and I were the only women in six- and eight-member troupes presenting razor-sharp political satire. She and I each worked many different jobs to support our art habits.

Suzy never passed up the chance to celebrate others, bringing flowers, streamers, jokes, soup, zany gifts, and handcrafted cards to her many loved ones. Her fashion sense knocked my socks off. Deeply spiritual and prophetic, Suzy also knew when to set aside slapstick and come forth with poems, prayers, and visual art to soothe life's pain.

Our collaborations began a couple of years after I started Amandla. I wanted to be like her: a leader who encourages collaboration as well as a friend who honors pain and loss.

Each time I direct our chorus, whether in rehearsal or in concert, Suzy's influence guides me. She's the main reason I'm committed to fostering a sense of family within the chorus, bringing forth deep bonds, hilarious moments, and the gentle tending of broken hearts.

I honor all of my exquisite mentors and teachers. The gospel music expert Dr. Horace Clarence Boyer encouraged and guided me through many collaborations. Dr. Ysaye Maria Barnwell, Sweet Honey in the Rock singer and masterful workshop leader, demonstrated to me the power of learning by ear. Pete Seeger's wit and wisdom are woven into my being.

But no one taught me more about art and the passionate life than Suzy Polucci. Without the touch of her grace, I would not be half the artist I am today.

The borrowed shirt

Retired physician Tom Plaut had a generous heart and a wicked sense of humor. Arriving for rehearsal one evening in 2002, he looked at his chorus mates and smacked his forehead. "We were supposed to wear costumes for the photo shoot. I blew it!" His button-down shirt was crisp and presentable but bore little resemblance to the bold, primary-color T-shirts of the usual chorus costume.

"Don't worry," I told Tom. "Some singers brought extra shirts and sashes in case others forgot."

"Good. I'll find one," said Tom, making his way through the crowd.

The photographer arrived, bringing an impressive array of lights and gadgets. She set up while we discussed ways to get optimal shots for promotional photos.

"All right, everyone," I called out. "Take your places for the shoot!" As usual, it was like herding cats. I overheard observations about flyaway hair. Some people removed eyeglasses. The singers helped each other even up the ends of the sashes that are part of our chorus's garb—strips of cloth from around the world, sewn together to symbolize that we belong together on our planet.

"Wear lipstick," Lori said loudly. "Otherwise, your lips will disappear in the photo!" This prompted a cascade of hilarious make-up application tips directed at the majority of singers who wore no make-up of any kind. The group went out of control once again.

"OK . . . c'mon . . . " I said, impatiently, aware that the clock was ticking on the photographer's time and we were wasting precious rehearsal minutes with a big show right around the corner.

I heard Tom's voice boom from the back row: "It nearly fits!" Holding clasped hands over his head in a gesture of victory, he demonstrated how the sleeves of the borrowed shirt came halfway down his forearms. Chorus members tittered.

But it wasn't until he stepped from behind a group of sopranos that we received the full impact. The shirt he borrowed from Marcia was a lovely V-neck. On Marcia, it looked tasteful and lovely. On Tom, however, the skin-tight fit and low neckline revealed much of Tom's hairy chest with tufts of thick grey and black hair sprouting every which way.

The photographer's mouth fell open as chorus members lost all sense of decorum. Singers doubled over howling and mopped their eyes with the ends of their sashes. Pure bedlam.

Hoo, boy, I thought. *Good luck reining them in.*

"Tom!" I said firmly, in a feeble attempt to demonstrate that I could regain control. "Stand in the back, will you?" I tried to sound businesslike but struggled to stifle my own laughter.

"Stand in the back, you say?" replied Tom in a jovial, taunting tone. "No need! I know just what to do!"

He whipped off the shirt and stood half naked, fit as a fiddle in his mid-seventies.

The chorus went wilder, shrieking with laughter that bounced off the beautifully crafted walls of Temple Israel, our rented rehearsal space since 2001. Tom tossed the borrowed shirt in the air, caught it with a flourish, and donned it once more — this time, backward.

The shirt was still skin tight, of course, and looked even more awkward in the new orientation. But Tom's chest hair was covered except for a few strands, which he attempted in faux modesty to tuck beneath the shirt.

"There," he said, with satisfaction, twirling around. "Better?"

It wasn't easy to get back on track, but the photographer got some shots and we rehearsed a few songs that evening.

As singers headed home, teen-aged Mari remarked, "Tom, you're the coolest old person I know."

To which Tom replied, "Thank you, Mari. I think you're a cool young person."

You liberated me

While keeping the music front and center, I experiment with ways to make time in rehearsals for singers to get to know one another. This can prove a fine line within the framework of two-hour, weekly sessions.

Singers find it enriching to share personal challenges or victories, especially if they wish to request support. We end rehearsals with the tried and true closing circle. While there's no pressure to do so, many members speak up in the circle at one time or another.

For years, I avoided such a model. In some contexts, a closing circle strikes me as awkward. Yet in our singing community, it is a central strand in our web of love and regard.

Mandy lets us know about the adoption process. Peter says he and his wife will attend two special events when their daughter graduates from high school in Greenfield and their son from Oberlin College in Ohio. Dina updates us on the status of Andrea, a former Amandla singer diagnosed with cancer.

Jody and I each ask for best wishes for our mothers, who've moved into assisted living facilities in neighboring towns. Michelle has a new kitten. Annie's daughter labors on the verge of birthing her second child.

Now and then, we devote part of a rehearsal to marking special occasions. We fête singers on landmark birthdays or create brief rituals, as we did when Alex and Joe awaited their first child.

In this spirit, Carol asked in the spring of 2009 if we could dedicate time within a rehearsal to celebrate the sixty-fifth wedding anniversary of her parents-in-law. Carol and her husband, Paul, wanted to bring his parents from Northampton so we could honor them with a few songs.

Paul brought his father and mother, Sandy and Phyllis, to our rehearsal. We sang for them, and Paul told a few stories about his parents.

Paul mentioned that his father, who at ninety was blind and quite frail, served in the Army's 106th Division during World War II. This got the attention of Diedrick, who at age seventy-eight was our oldest singer at the time. Born in 1931 in the Netherlands, Diedrick lived under Nazi occupation for several years as a child.

"Where in Europe did you serve?" Diedrick asked with great interest. Paul conferred with his father, who spoke in a very soft voice. Paul reported the names of several places. Diedrick gasped, and everyone turned toward him. Visibly shaken, Diedrick rose to his feet and walked slowly across the space that separated him from the older couple. He attempted to speak, but his voice faltered. He knelt before Sandy and took the older man's hands in both of his.

Diedrick managed to speak. "You . . . Sir . . . you liberated me. Thank you." His voice quieted to a whisper. "Thank you," he repeated. He remained while Paul explained the connection to his dad.

Lifting his head and fixing his sightless gaze in Diedrick's direction, Sandy deliberately raised a hand and, finding Diedrick's shoulder, placed his hand there in recognition and solidarity.

I wondered if we should honor the moment with a solemn and meaningful song. I came up with nothing suitable. Even if I'd been able to think of one, there's no chance the singers could have produced sounds other than weeping and nose-blowing.

We wept quietly as two magnificent elders who had shared space far across the sea when they were twenty-six and fourteen years of age remained in a loving stance that defied fascism and the ravages of time. They showed us how to celebrate true liberty and our common humanity.

Homesick

Eager to hear about anti-apartheid work, southern Vermonters filled every seat of the Guilford Community Church on Lincoln's birthday, 1989.

We began with "Freedom Is Coming." Southern Vermont crowds eagerly sing along in their regional hotbed of music, thanks to gifted songsters including Mary Cay Brass, Andy Davis, and Peter and Mary Alice Amidon.

After several rousing songs, we settled into the lush harmonies of "Thuma Mina," a call and response song in Zulu meaning "Send me, Spirit." The crowd, quiet and intent, soaked up the richly reverent, repeated lines.

I heard a sound from the back of the church. It began at medium volume and soon reached a greater level. *A crying baby?* I guessed. I scanned the room for an infant but then realized the sound was pitched too low for a child's voice.

I located the source. Eyes closed, a woman in the last row swayed. Her moaning stopped each time she inhaled deeply, then resumed and wove its way into the song. Her moans changed to a repeated, plaintive word: "Homesick." Coming from this beautiful South African woman, the word sounded like *Homm-seek! Homm-seek!* It filled the room.

Should we stop? I wondered. *Is this song causing too much pain?* A glance at the singers, older and wiser than I, revealed unanimous instruction: Do *not* shy away from this sacred moment.

That became my first humbling experience of evoking deep feeling from audience members who recognize sounds or songs in an intimate way.

When I met the lovely, strong woman after the program, I learned painful and inspiring things about her life growing up in white-dominated South Africa as well as some of her struggles in coming to the US to study.

By sharing the depths of her longing and sorrow, she reminded us that each song must be considered a living thing treated with respect and recognition of its sacred role in the community. A freedom song represents far more than a performance piece. As a common thread of our international family, such songs help us see that—as long as injustice can take root anywhere to compromise dignity—homesickness affects us all.

Hospice singing

Our chorus members love to sing for and with people in public spaces. Yet there's another way we share our music and our hearts, one that touches us deeply every time.

When invited to bring a few singers into private homes, hospital rooms, and hospices, we enter into sacred relationships with individuals and families. Such intensely personal visits are among the greatest gifts of our experience.

We offer two types of intimate visits: one to encourage those recovering from illness or surgery, the other to offer solace and peace at or near life's end.

Many articles and books explore the topic of singing for people in hospice settings. I urge readers who wish to engage in that sacred activity to consult the wisdom and research of others, including Kathy Leo in southern Vermont. It's important to learn from experienced practitioners and those who study the topic extensively. I do not claim to be an expert by any stretch, despite some training.

One Sunday afternoon, five of us sang in a two-hundred-year-old farmhouse for a woman stricken by ALS, also known as Lou Gehrig's Disease. I'd heard of the disease but never witnessed its effects.

During our warmup outside the home, singers shared concerns about singing for a dying woman and her family. *How will we stay on pitch and focus on the lyrics? If we experience or witness intense emotions, can we keep going? What will happen if we start to cry?*

"We'll do our best," I told the singers as we reviewed basic agreements related to hospice work.

We greeted the woman and her family. The only sounds were the ticking clock and hissing woodstove. "Swing down, Chariot" took on new meaning as we sang, "I got a home on the other side." We knew the woman who would soon leave her loved ones and home. We had talked and joked with her over the years and seen her at work in a favorite public venue. We knew her kids. Although her mind and emotions functioned as before the onset of illness, at the time of our visit she could barely speak and moved only her head.

The song ended with a final repetition of "I got a home on the other side," and the woman began to cry. She cried honestly and openly in a way that's available to some people nearing the end of physical life and who meet death without flinching. She glowed as she wept.

Painstakingly, she said, "Beautiful!" Then, "More!" Her kind, loving husband beamed as his own tears flowed.

She said "More!" after every song. The session that began with tentative sadness ended with holy sweetness.

She was tired and could make no more sounds. But her mouth shaped the words, "Thank you . . . thank you."

We felt light and impermanent as we bade farewell to that beautiful family. We became acutely aware that our times, too, would come.

At her funeral, I sang Dougie MacLean's "This Love Will Carry Me."

A little girl and a big chorus

In 1992, I met an extraordinary seven-year-old South African girl named Amandla who brought immense joy to my life from the moment I met her.

I recalled when a South African friend suggested the chorus choose the name Amandla because the Zulu word meaning power occurs in many South African freedom songs.

The little girl's parents worked with the African National Congress (ANC) and wanted to give their daughter a powerful name. The child who joined our community in western Massachusetts was one of the most powerful people I had ever met of any age or size.

The Reverend Fred Emerick, pastor of the Saint James Episcopal Church in Greenfield, greeted me over the phone. What he said astonished me, and I asked him to repeat it.

Neo and Amandla shortly after arriving in Greenfield, 1992

"I thought you'd be interested in knowing that a South African woman just moved to Greenfield. She fled a violent situation and moved here two weeks ago with two children. One of the children is named Amandla." He gave me the woman's name and a number where I could reach her.

When I called Mapula, she sounded wary. I introduced myself, welcomed her to Greenfield, and asked if I could do anything to help her and the children. I added, "I direct a community chorus called Amandla. We sing South African freedom songs."

She asked me to repeat the last part and then said, "There's a choir called Amandla here singing South African freedom songs?"

I invited Mapula to our next rehearsal. She said she would come. I found it amazing that a woman fleeing a violent situation with two children, one of whom had a serious heart defect, felt willing to meet strangers.

Mapula later told me that a politically active friend had been murdered at Mapula's home near Johannesburg and that she'd fled because she no longer knew whom to trust. It's a testimony to the human spirit that she came to our rehearsal, bringing the children with her and planting seeds of friendship.

As we finished the song "Singabahambayo," Mapula entered our rehearsal space with her arms protectively around the children: seven-year-old Amandla and eight-year-old Neo, whose name means gift. Mapula introduced Neo as her youngest son and Amandla as the daughter of her best friend. Neo seemed particularly shy. Neo and Amandla stared quizzically at North American adults singing South African freedom songs.

The little girl did not know that her father's murder was the reason Mapula and the children fled to the US. Hoping to escape his fate, the dead man's family scattered in different directions. Mapula worked hard to keep the children safe and happy. She did not tell them about the murder.

Our visitors sat listening in a pew. When we began "Nkosi Sikelel' iAfrika," the anthem of the ANC and of freedom-loving people throughout Africa, the little girl slipped out of the pew and stood with us, her small fist thrust in the air, eyes closed. She sang with her head tipped back. When we finished the song and did the call-and-response chant, she grinned and said, "Sing more." So we sang.

Over the next few months, I spent a lot of time with my new friends. The children attended school at Federal Street Elementary and picked up English rapidly. I helped them with schoolwork, and in return, they tutored me in their native language, Sotho.

"Dumela, o kae?" (Hello, how are you?)

"Keteng wena o kae." (I'm fine. How are you?)

The children tried not to giggle at my attempts.

One phrase I learned quickly and used frequently was "Etla mo" (Come on.) During our outings, the children often became fixated on the smallest things, especially at the World Eye Bookshop. Sometimes I needed to repeat "Etla" several times so shopkeepers could close up and go home.

Outings ended with a beautiful phrase: "Katla ho bona hosane" (I'll see you tomorrow).

One day, Amandla taught me a new phrase as she sat in my lap: "Ke thabile." (I am happy.) We repeated it many times.

Mapula sounded upset one wintry day after speaking to Amandla's mother on the phone. "We have to send Amandla back," Mapula told me. "I don't know how we're going to do it, but we must."

My hand gripped the phone.

Mapula explained that the family sent Amandla, the youngest of seven children and therefore considered the most vulnerable, overseas immediately following her father's murder. The family withheld the facts, telling her only that she would have a lovely trip and come home soon.

"Things have settled down for the family, at least for the moment," Mapula added. "Her mother wants her back. It's time for her to hear the truth, and they must tell her in person."

I rationalized in the face of the understandable request: *She's thriving, she's in a good school, she's safe.* Yet my resistance was selfish. I didn't want to let go of her beautiful presence in my life. When I thought of the girl's family, though, I knew we had to send her home.

I told Mapula, "We'll figure this out. The chorus will do a benefit concert to raise money for a plane ticket."

I hung up the phone and wept.

The night of the benefit, it was standing room only at the Shea Theater in Turners Falls. The news had spread both by word of mouth and in a big story in the *Greenfield Recorder*, the community's daily newspaper.

Amandla insisted on coming on stage to sing with the chorus that shared her name. I asked if she was sure, explaining that there would be lots of people in the audience, and stage lights are very bright. "I want to," she said forcefully. Photos of that evening show a determined child waist-high to the adults around her.

We raised enough funds for a plane ticket and spending money.

The airline staff impressed me. We explained to Amandla that her plane would fly first to London, where she could play with other kids in a day care center while waiting twelve hours for her next plane. As we packed and re-packed her bags, I realized there's no way to prepare to let go of such a child.

And then she was gone.

We lost contact with her. Mapula tracked her down once by calling a relative's home and waiting while someone fetched Amandla from another house.

When Amandla finally came to the phone, she was crying. "Please, Mama Mapula! Come get me! There's not enough to eat, and I have no good clothes to go to school!"

After the call, Mapula and I sat overwhelmed by helplessness for a long time.

Sometimes when I think of her, my throat tightens while singing and no sound comes out. Then I remember the joy in her voice as she sat in my lap and said "Ke thabile. Ke thabile."

Wherever she is, may her spirit be strong.

Mandela

Following my cashier shift at the food co-op, I walked three blocks to my efficiency apartment carrying groceries. I needed to get some items into the fridge on a warm Monday afternoon in 1990.

Pushing the door open with my elbow, I heaved cloth bags onto the counter as the phone rang.

"Is this Emily MacDonald, director of the singing group?" a man asked.

"It's Eveline MacDougall, but, yes," I replied.

"Alright, Ms. McDoodle." He quickly introduced himself with a name I didn't catch. "Can your chorus come to Boston this Saturday to sing at the Hatch Shell? We're staging a public event to welcome Nelson Mandela. We're expecting upwards of two hundred thousand people."

Oh, those hilarious Amandla singers, I thought. *Such pranksters! I wonder which one this is? I don't recognize the voice right off . . .*

"Ohhhh, suuuuure," I played along with a goofy voice. "That sounds SO fun! And maybe next weekend we can sing for Jesus and Mohammed on the moon! Ha, ha! Sign us up!"

There was silence on the other end, then a sigh. "You think this is a joke? Well, it's not. Peter, Paul, and Mary are still in Europe on tour and can't make it back in time. I need to fill this slot." As though speaking to himself, he added, "It's beyond me why we even need another act, since we already have Stevie Wonder, Paul Simon, Tracy Chapman, Ladysmith, Jackson Browne . . . "

I gulped.

"But, hell . . . OK. You don't want to do it? I'll see if I can get some local school group or something. They want a big group for the end after Mandela gives his speech. Well, thanks anyway."

"Wait," I yelled. "Wait, wait. Please. I'm so sorry. I thought this was a prank. Can we start over?"

He laughed. "Sure."

"This is for real?" I asked, wanting to make sure.

"Yeah, it's real. You in?"

"Sir," I replied, my mind spinning. "I. Am. In."

He speed-rapped instructions, saying I had forty-eight hours to fax the state department names and social security numbers of all participants. This was before the internet. Singers from outside the US must produce other forms of documentation.

"Get me the complete list by Wednesday at this time, or it's a no-go." I scribbled his fax number and repeated it. "That's right," he confirmed. "Wednesday, or you're out. Got it?"

"Got it," I said, and he hung up.

I put the dairy products in the fridge and began dialing. I could've farmed out some of the calls by using the chorus phone tree, but it was way too much fun to hear reactions from people I reached directly.

I called members of Amandla and Barwa as well as Noonday Singers and a few Pioneer Valley musicians I considered ringers. I wanted a BIG SOUND for Mr. Mandela and two hundred thousand people.

The Cambridge Friends Meeting graciously allowed us to use their space that June Saturday morning so we could rehearse before heading to the big stage.

As we rehearsed, I thought about how the South African singers had grown up revering Mandela while living with the reality that his image and words were banned as he lived confined to a South African prison. Newspapers could not legally carry his photo, statements, health status, legal situation, or background. Excitement filled each singer that day, but our South African friends exuded disbelief, gratitude, and pride.

Will I ever love an American leader the way they – the way we all – revere Mandela? Will the US ever have a pivotal figure, a tireless freedom fighter and beacon of hope like Mandela is for South Africans?

Then I remembered heroes like Alice Walker, Howard Zinn, Frances Crowe, Wally and Juanita Nelson, Daniel Berrigan. All nations have great souls.

The singers filled the Meetinghouse with songs and stories until it was time to proceed to the Hatch Shell.

We witnessed Boston neighborhoods gloriously mad with Mandela Fever. People of all ages, shapes, sizes, and skin shades thronged the streets sporting Mandela T-shirts and placards. The city felt like a joyful, cross-cultural party.

Some singers who knew Boston well spoke of the city's reputation for being hostile to people of color. Yet on this day, people from many backgrounds and ethnicities turned out to see Mandela, an international icon. Could one man change hearts with one visit?

Police officers halted our vans and cars at a checkpoint. They instructed us to proceed on foot beyond barricades designating a safe zone around the performance area. Once we stepped into restricted territory, cops on horseback escorted us.

Large tents sported VIP labels. *From banned prisoner to Very Important Person,* I mused. Imprisoned for the so-called crime of advocating for basic human rights, Mandela spent nearly thirty years on South Africa's Robben Island, separated from loved ones. In Boston, he was surrounded by police officers intent on preserving his safety. The enormity hit me in waves.

I slackened my pace, causing singers behind me to slow down, too. An officer astride a beautiful, clip-clopping horse snapped me out of it: "Step it UP, there!" he shouted, pointing his baton at me. A quarter of a million people waited.

He escorted us to a tent with folding chairs, tables, and a small television showing the onstage action. Governor Michael Dukakis greeted Mandela: "Though you were an ocean away, we in Massachusetts have been at your side. Today you are greeted by hundreds of thousands of people to whom you have brought hope and inspiration and a sense of what is possible when a love of freedom knows no fear."

Musical performances punctuated speeches. We peeked beyond the stage at the crowd: humans, balloons, and festive colors as far as the eye could see along the Charles River on a gorgeous summer day.

Some of our singers chatted with Paul Simon while others met up with members of Ladysmith Black Mambazo, the iconic South African group featuring relatives and colleagues of Joseph Shabalala, the group's founder.

Some people think Ladysmith became well known due to their work with Paul Simon. Although associating with Simon expanded their audience, the pitch-perfect, athletic group won competitions and delighted fans since the 1960s.

The musical legends were every bit as friendly and easy-going as they appear onstage. I learned that the group's name represents three elements: Ladysmith is Shabalala's hometown in the KwaZulu-Natal region, the black ox was known as the strongest farm animal, and mambazo means axe in Zulu, symbolizing the choir's ability to chop down the competition.

"Yikes," quipped one of our singers, "I'm glad we're not competing with you!"

A young Ladysmith member teased, "We'll take you on! LET'S GO!" We declined, and everyone laughed. I loved watching folks from Barwa chat with their fellow South Africans. We parted with handshakes and hugs as Ladysmith members headed back to their tent.

Singers elbowed each other when other luminaries walked by. After a while, a combination of the day's warmth and lack of sleep left me feeling woozy. When the actor Danny Glover came to our tent, "looking for the choral director," I felt tongue-tied and drowsy.

In his famously deep, resonant voice, Glover said, "I've been asked to introduce your chorus. Is there anything in particular you'd like me to say?"

"We're a conglomeration of Amandla, Barwa, the Noonday Singers, and a few others to help make the sound as big as possible . . . ," I stammered.

On stage at the Hatch Shell, Boston, June 23, 1990

My mind wandered as I recalled phoning singers to let them know of the invitation to participate in this historic event.

Mr. Glover brought me back with a gentle throat-clearing sound. Poised to write on a small card, he said, "How about I just say the first two names—Amandla and Barwa, right? How do you spell that? Where are you from?"

I listed singers' places of origin. He smiled. "I'll just say western Massachusetts and South Africa." Raising an eyebrow, he added, "Sounds like an interesting group!"

Ted Kennedy walked by. Someone spotted Tracy Chapman. Hoping to meet Stevie Wonder, we craned our necks.

New commotion stirred. "He's LEAVING," someone said plaintively.

"Who?" I asked, feeling really out of it. "Who's leaving?"

"Mr. Mandela," wailed a member of Barwa. She looked bereft. "He's not yet heard us sing!"

Darn. We don't even get to pay him tribute in person! I consoled myself with the thought: *At least there's still tens of thousands of people in the audience.*

A limo with tinted windows crawled through the crowd. I made a guess as to who was inside. I shouted to the singers, "To the limo! Nkosi Sikelel'i!" The title of the anthem spread quickly amongst the singers. Moving toward the limo while singing the opening lines, we formed a tight group.

The limo lurched to a halt, and the back door flew open. He strode toward us with a grin, fist in the air. Bodyguards scrambled to surround Mandela, but he moved into our group, joining the song. Men with dark glasses and thin wires running from their ears to beneath their shirt collars surrounded our group and watched our every move.

At the last chord, Mandela's voice rang out: "AMANDLA!" to which we jubilantly responded: "Ngawethu!"

*Outside the Hatch Shell, Boston, shortly after Amandla sang
"Nkosi Sikelel' iAfrika" with Nelson Mandela as the singers
erupted into joyful dance and song after Mandela's limo pulled away*

We were thrilled to share the rallying call-and-response chant
of the ANC and its allies. The Zulu and Xhosa word Amandla,
meaning power, is answered: "It is ours." We'd done it many
times in concert and at public protests, but to experience it with
Nelson Mandela was overwhelming.

After greeting us and shaking many hands, Mr. Mandela was ushered back to the limo by security detail. A weary-looking Winnie Mandela sat in the limo. They had to press on in their eight-city, twelve-day tour.

The purpose of the tour was twofold. Mandela wanted to express gratitude to activists who supported the struggle against apartheid rule in South Africa. In 1982, Massachusetts was the first state to withdraw pension funds from companies doing business in South Africa. Mandela said publicly it was a particular joy to thank the Bay State.

He and other ANC leaders had another task, as well. They worked to move South Africa from white domination to a democratically elected government. We heard Mandela hoped to raise a minimum of one million dollars from each city on his US tour in order to fund the election process.

As the limo pulled away, I looked to the singers—especially Mzamo, Menzi, Thami, Mohapi, Prudence, Mpho, Anil, Verna, and Sifa—who had roots in South AFrica. I looked to their faces for proof that we'd really sung "Nkosi Sikelel' iAfrika" with Mr. Mandela.

The proof was there in shining faces streaked with tears. We hadn't even gone on stage yet, but the day couldn't possibly get better. We erupted into drumming, dancing, hooting, singing, hugging, and elation.

An event organizer told us to head to the stage, where we sang our hearts out to the massive crowd. Precious moments with Mr. Mandela inspired us to sing like we'd never sung.

Within four years, the former political prisoner became South Africa's first Black president.

Amandla ngawethu!

A Hero's Welcome

*Finally, a hero for our times. Nelson Mandela hits
the streets of New England*

PHOTO BY EDWARD COHEN/AFRICAN COMMENTARY

Nelson and Winnie Mandela at Madison Park High School, Boston

By Stephanie Kraft

In South Africa, conservative opposition to the government's reforms is ominous and building. Whites talk of killing, or dying, rather than being ruled by a black majority. Nominal as the de Klerk reforms may seem—how much did it cost the government to free Nelson Mandela anyway?—they have pro-apartheid Afrikaners talking of apocalypse. Last week one such family told the *Wall Street Journal*, "The most popular video in South africa today is the release of Mandela. You just play it backwards."

In America, even Nelson Mandela—after 27 years of confinement the archetypal political prisoner of all time—finds that he cannot use the word "nationalize" without the landmines of Cold War semantics blowing up in his face. And, even as Mandela reminds Americans why it is important to maintain sanctions against South

AMANDLA GREETS MANDELA

For Western Mass.' Amandla ("power" in Zulu) Choir, Nelson Mandela's visit to Boston was unforgettable.

Amandla, a multiracial chorus whose 60 members have been gathering in Franklin county to sing South African freedom songs for more than two years, enthusiastically sent a tape to the organizers of the music for the Mandela appearance early in the game. Then they realized that the acts lined up for the afternoon—Jackson Browne, Paul Simon, Michelle Shocked—were big-time professionals.

But just six days before the Mandela visit, Amandla leader Eveline McDougall got the surprise of her life when Tom Bates, who staged-managed the June 23 concert for the Don Law Agency in Cambridge, called her to tell her Amandla was on the program. The catch: All the singers had to send their birthdays and social security numbers to the State Department for security clearance. No one who couldn't do it in time could enter the Hatch Shell at the Esplanade. The screening eliminated about 10 Amandla regulars who couldn't be reached in time, McDougall said. But singers from Noonday Farm in Winchendon and Barwa, a Five College South African chorus, filled in.

When Nelson Mandela's motorcade arrive to the cheers of 250,000 people at the Esplanade, Amandla was there, scheduled to sing after his speech, which began at 6:15. The group went on stage 7:30, following Najee, as tens of thousands lingered on the Esplanade to relax in the twilight. As Mandela's limousine moved away from the Hatch Shell, Amandla sang "Nkosi Sikelel 'iAfrika" ("God Bless Africa"), the anthem of the African National Congress.

Nobody

Before Mandela's speech and hot on the heels of my brief chat with Danny Glover at the Mandela event, I stood outside the tent to get my bearings. Holding a clipboard and wearing large sunglasses, a man appeared. He grabbed my right hand, pumped it, and said, "It's great to finally meet you!"

"Really?" I said.

"Yeah! I'm a big fan!"

BS detectors in my head went off loudly.

"A fan of . . . ?" I prompted.

Checking his clipboard, he replied, "Um, A-MAN-dla." He mispronounced the word by rhyming the middle syllable with the word can.

"And you are?" I asked, knowing full well from his badge that he represented a well-known company that makes running shoes.

He introduced himself and spoke rapidly in a smooth voice. "I love what your group stands for," he said, peering at me over his shades. "Just love this whole freedom vibe. You folks are changing the world with your songs."

I nodded. "Yes, it's amazing to change the world. A wonderful way to spend the day."

Oblivious to my sarcasm, he said, "We have millions of customers who believe in what we're doing here today." He gestured toward the stage. "They'd love to see that your group is on the same page with their . . . freedom struggles."

"Your customers are struggling for freedom?" I asked in an alarmed tone. "Do you think they'll make it?"

He looked stymied and tried to clarify. "I mean, we're all in this together. I'd be honored if you sign with our company. I wanna schedule a photo shoot of your singers wearing our product. We'll make the shoot really fun and, for your trouble, you'll receive ten thousand dollars. In fact, I can cut you a check right now." Leaning toward me, he added, "I have the authority to do so."

"Hold on," I said, stepping back. "You're saying our chorus will get a check for ten thousand dollars if I agree to put my singers in your running shoes for a promotional ad?"

"It's an endorsement," he corrected me. "It's on the up and up. Think of the exposure your group will receive in addition to the generous remuneration."

"Oh, I'm thinking, I'm thinking," I replied. I tried to peek at his clipboard, but he hugged it to his chest. I asked, "How'd you hear about us?"

"Man, you kidding? You guys are . . . I'm so glad I get to hear you live!" His eyes darted, scoping the scene for fresher, more promising meat.

"You have a list of performers, don't you?" I pried. "We're listed right after Mandela speaks, aren't we?"

"This is HUGE," he replied, with forced enthusiasm. "Mandela is SO COOL."

"Lemme help you out," I said in a chummy tone. His eyes lit up.

I leaned in and whispered, "We're nobody."

His face went blank. "Whaddaya mean, nobody?"

I said it again, this time in a regular voice: "We're nobody."

"But . . . you're here," he insisted. "You can't be nobody."

"Trust me," I said. "We're nobody."

Losing all pretense of being a fan, he demanded, "Then what the hell are you doing here?"

"That . . . is SUCH . . . a great question!" I shouted with a grin. "We're here because Peter, Paul, and Mary couldn't make it back from Europe in time to do the show. We got in because we sing South African songs! Isn't that fantastic? We're having the time of our lives, but we're not gonna sell sneakers for you!"

He looked embarrassed. I tapped his clipboard. "Listen, pal, do you know how many people are in my group?"

He stepped back and shrugged. "I dunno. Eight or ten, like them?" He pointed toward Ladysmith's tent.

"Nah," I said. "Try fifty-five."

"Fifty-five!" he gasped.

"Yup! That's a lot of sneakers, right?" I nodded. "When they get back from Europe, maybe Peter, Paul, and Mary would lace up your sneakers and sell product? That's only six shoes."

"Wait," he said. "Do you know them?"

"No," I said, and reminded him, "I told you. We're nobody. But today?" I cackled, "Today, we're feeling pretty cool."

One of the singers signaled that Mandela's speech was about to begin.

"Hey, good luck with the sneakers," I said to my ex-fan and headed into the tent to hear a man who never set off my BS detector.

"Who was that?" a friend asked.

"Him?" I said, chuckling. "Nobody."

Pete Seeger

Pete Seeger mentored scores of musicians and activists over many years. I feel lucky to be among those who benefited from his generous guidance.

Finishing a full afternoon of teaching piano lessons in 1997, I wanted nothing other than to sit quietly on the porch. The phone rang.

Let the machine pick it up. Oh, heck. I'll answer.

"Eveline? It's Pete."

Over the twenty-five years I knew the beloved songwriter and organizer, I enjoyed every moment of his mentoring — much of which took place by mail and over the phone.

I led a workshop at the 1990 Peoples' Music Network (PMN) summer gathering in New York State. I taught "Qula Kwedini," a rite-of-passage song I learned from my friends in Barwa.

Someone arrived late and slipped into the bass section. Within minutes, the latecomer interjected insightful questions. I turned to face him. My stomach flip-flopped. Pete Seeger stood in my singing workshop. As he posed astute questions about intricate time signatures, I regained my balance.

I often feel awe in meeting people who inspire me, but that grey summer afternoon was the last time I ever felt "less than" while interacting with a famous person. Pete demonstrated the importance of working with others on projects, songs, and ideas.

Pete Seeger performing at the Clearwater Festival,
Croton Point Park, New York, June, 1994 just before Amandla took the stage

Three years after that PMN workshop, Amandla singers boarded a chartered bus in Greenfield and headed for Manhattan's West Sixty-Second Street. We were pumped! On the road, Amandla always has high energy, but never before had our destination been Lincoln Center.

Pete hatched a plan to bring what he called a Coalition of Choruses to Damrosch Park, Lincoln Center's outdoor stage. He asked if I would lead a couple of songs. Not wanting to overstep but not wanting to miss an opportunity, I hesitantly asked if I could bring my whole chorus. "Sure!" said Pete. "The more, the merrier!"

Arriving in Manhattan, I caught up with Pete amid preparatory onstage chaos. He looked tired, having planned the event with characteristic zeal. "You get any sleep last night, Pete?" I asked.

"Hardly any!" he said. "I was up most of the night making the banner."

"The banner?" I wondered aloud.

"The banner!" he crowed, pointing to a group of volunteers unrolling a sheet about three feet high and many feet long. Covered in colorful, hand-lettered words, the banner stretched across the stage with a stick on each end.

I recognized the oversized words as the refrain from a well-known song: "Y por eso los grandes amores de muchos colores me gustan a mí." The Mexican folk song, "De Colores," often associated with the United Farm Workers, is included in many international folk song collections.

The refrain, which Pete transformed into an enormous work of art, can be translated in a number of ways, including: "And that is why the great loves of many colors are pleasing to me."

Many singing groups from the metropolitan area made up the Coalition of Choruses.

Amandla contributed two songs, "Freedom Is Coming" and "Siyahamba," to the potluck song event.

Each choral director had only weeks to prep their singers for the innovative concert. We struggled to learn songs in Spanish, Zulu, Irish Gaelic, Turkish, Hebrew, Sotho, and English. We learned as best we could during our summer break, and our most intensive rehearsal occurred that very day on the bus en route from Greenfield to Manhattan.

When the time came for Amandla's contributions, I took my place facing the combined choruses, with three thousand people sitting behind me in the audience. Before raising the pitch pipe to my lips, I feasted my eyes on a couple hundred singers of all conceivable shapes, sizes, ages, skin shades, abilities, and cultural backgrounds.

He's done it again. He dreams of our Rainbow Family and then makes it happen. I gave the starting note and the huge choir erupted in joyful sound. All of the choruses, except for Amandla, were from the metropolitan area.

Onstage, we became one voice.

Halfway through the show, volunteers paraded the banner up and down the aisles so members of the capacity crowd could join in, which they did, at the tops of their lungs.

One glance at Pete revealed that he didn't regret one moment of lost sleep. *This is what he lives for!*

In June, 1994, Pete invited Amandla to sing at another exhilarating event, the Clearwater Festival in Croton Point Park, New York.

Pete phoned from time to time during the late 1990s, usually with this opener: "I'm not supposed to sing. Strict orders. Somehow, I wore out my voice. But I can whistle! Do you know this song?"

TOSHI & PETER SEEGER
BOX 431, BEACON, N. Y. 12508

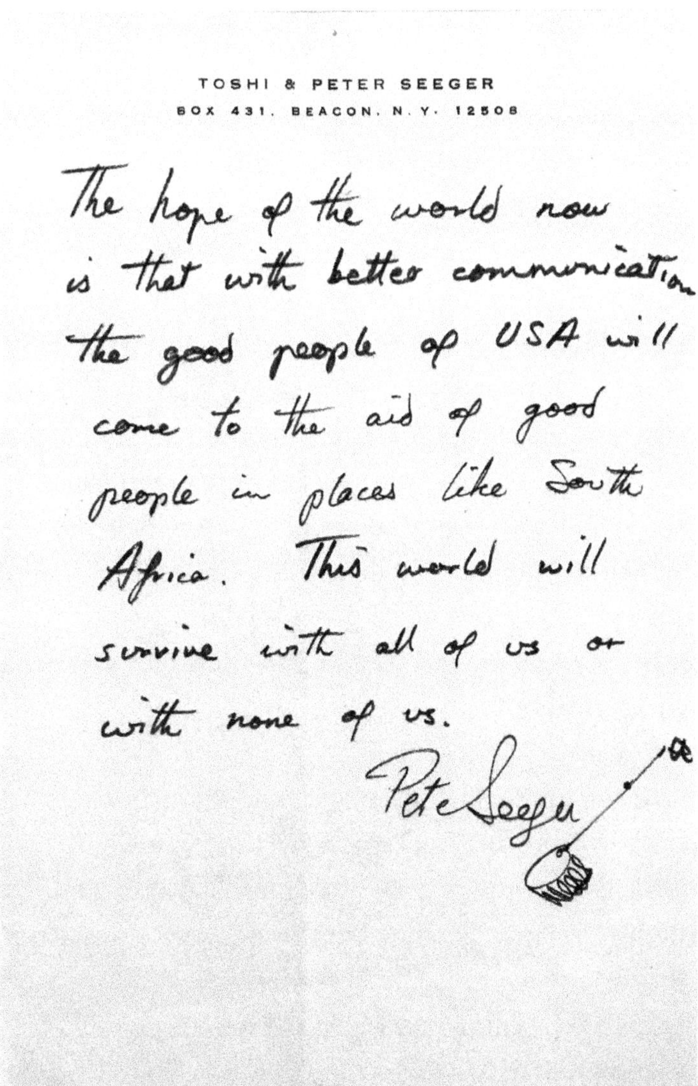

The hope of the world now is that with better communication the good people of USA will come to the aid of good people in places like South Africa. This world will survive with all of us or with none of us.

Pete Seeger

PRINTED ON RECYCLED PAPER

A note Pete sent Eveline about activism and South Africa in the early 1990s

In sharing songs, Pete also encouraged me to improvise harmonies. I passed many a pleasant, awkward hour holding the mouthpiece in normal position while holding the earpiece several inches from my ear to compensate for the piercing nature of whistling.

I listened to Pete's melody line while staring out the window at late afternoon traffic. I forget which song he demonstrated that day through pursed lips; I recall, however, that one passage got my attention. "Pete, could you do that a few more times?"

He obliged. Experimenting with various harmonies, I hummed with the mouthpiece far from my mouth. I found a groove as Pete kept up the melody. Bringing my mouth closer to the phone, I hummed more confidently. Pete stopped. "Do that again, please?" he requested.

I did so. I guessed from his wavering whistle that he was nodding. "Hold the phone, please," he said, breathlessly. "Alright, I've got staff paper and pencil. Once again."

I hummed my harmony twice more. Pete asked, "Can I use this harmony?"

I laughed. "Pete! I've used your harmonies for years! Of course you can use it!"

He chuckled. "A trade, then."

"Well, if we're trading," I said, "I owe you dozens."

"Good!" he said. "Talk to you next time!" *Click.*

Our whistling sessions generally lasted about an hour, punctuated by historical context and stories. What initially seemed an odd way to use the telephone became some of my favorite moments with Pete, adding richly to the foundation I gleaned from my association with this brilliant and generous man.

The course of my life was greatly influenced in 1991 during a weekend sojourn to the Seeger home in Beacon, New York.

That unforgettable visit showed me there would be no Seeger phenomenon without the talents of Toshi, Pete's driven, efficient wife.

Initially, I felt intimidated by Toshi. She moved with purpose and could cut to the quick. I hadn't yet learned that her brisk manner was the hallmark of a brilliant woman who had the ability to juggle many projects without dropping balls while managing one of the world's most sought-after artists. Pete would have drowned in requests and been hog-tied by the calendar had it not been for Toshi's abilities. Her husband—generous to a fault—felt he should say "Yes" to virtually everything. Toshi's cool head and razor-sharp instincts kept them on an even keel, which shouldn't be surprising coming from the woman who taught Pete to sail.

The Seeger kitchen buzzed with family, friends, and the chopping of vegetables. Toshi assembled an enormous salad. The phone rang yet again, and Pete looked as if the instrument might bite him. He picked it up and listened while staring at the ceiling. Narrowing his eyes, he said, "I see. When?" He repeated the date. "That's a good project. Yes, I think I could do a short set."

"PETER!" interjected Toshi. "We have a Clearwater meeting that day!"

"Ah," Pete told his caller. "Toshi reminds me we have an engagement on that date. I'm so sorry. Perhaps next time?"

Never missing a beat while slicing carrots, Toshi blew a strand of hair from her eyes.

"See what I deal with?" she exclaimed. Yet a moment later, she smiled discreetly. Pete shrugged. I recognized an unbeatable team.

Early the next morning, the kitchen was quiet, but Pete knew it was a temporary lull. "I invited you here so we can talk about important things," he said. "Around here, it's easier to talk outside." Leaving the newer house, we walked to a spot behind the family's original cabin, which they'd built themselves.

Although I'd grown less star-struck, on this Sunday morning I felt shy around a man I considered a hero.

Pete meandered through a few stories about traveling with the folk singer Woody Guthrie. I drank in every word. Finishing a story, Pete grew quiet. He broke the silence with a deep sigh.

"I envy your life. Tax resistance strikes me as the most sensible choice in a world gone mad with warring. I wish I had the courage to do it. Forrest Gump put me in a whole new tax bracket. But you've got the right idea."

The hit movie featured one of Pete's songs, "Turn, Turn, Turn."

I noted to Pete that the income I earned as a self-employed musician, supplemented by side-jobs, kept me in an income bracket below taxation. "I do that on purpose," I added.

Pete said, "You're nearly guaranteed that bracket as a self-employed musician!" We chuckled, but his smile vanished as he tapped the picnic table once with each emphatic word, "Don't. Get. Famous."

"What do you mean?" I asked.

"It's complicated," he admitted. "Being well-known opens doors, but it gets hectic with too many requests and commitments. I'd love to work on a smaller scale, but the calendar takes on a life of its own."

I heard a door open and close. Toshi made her way toward us carrying a plate covered with a tea towel. "Blueberry muffins," she said briskly. "Fresh from the oven." With that, she headed back to the newer house.

Pete lifted the towel to reveal four steaming muffins along with several pats of butter and a small spreader. Toshi thought of everything, as usual.

"She bears the brunt of it," he said. "I couldn't do it without her, but I'm difficult to manage. I say yes to everything, more than I should, and she tries to keep me in line because it's not sustainable!"

He described Toshi's phenomenal organizational skills and many artistic talents.

"She's a force of nature," he said, shaking his head with an admiring smile.

Suddenly, I felt like an intruder in a private home. I suggested to Pete that perhaps I should head back to Massachusetts a little earlier than planned in order to give his family some privacy.

"No!" he exclaimed. "I invited you. I need to spend time with young folks, artists who move in the direction I want to go." He added, almost under his breath, "What I wouldn't give to trade lives with you for awhile. Directing that wonderful chorus, working in the community but without the fame and pressure."

We ate delicious muffins while Pete looked at the Hudson.

"I worry," he said, grimly. "What will become of us on this path of greed and militarism? Madness! We could turn it around if we prioritized education, art, gardens, cooperation." He looked at me. "Couldn't we?"

I didn't answer. Pete insisted, "We could."

In a low voice, he said, "Don't give up. Keep doing your chorus, and keep involving the community. Please stay in touch with me because what you're doing — what we're doing — might save our world."

I didn't say anything. He challenged me more directly: "Don't give it up."

I had not consciously decided to devote my life to leading the Amandla Chorus. I was twenty-five years old, with only two years invested in Amandla. Yet something in me shifted when Pete made his request.

I answered him, slowly: "I won't, Pete. I won't give it up." The moment I said it out loud, it felt right.

"Good!" he said. "You give me hope."

A little off balance at first, he unfolded his tall, thin frame from the picnic table. "Better not sit around all day." With the vigor of a man half his age, he said, "Let's split wood. We can talk as we work. You know how to split wood?"

I told him I learned while living with Wally and Juanita Nelson.

"Good," he said. "It's important to do real work." Collecting the plate containing only crumbs, he strode toward the house.

I followed Pete. I would follow Pete, gladly, many times in years to come.

Pete. What a blessing in my life — and in the lives of millions.

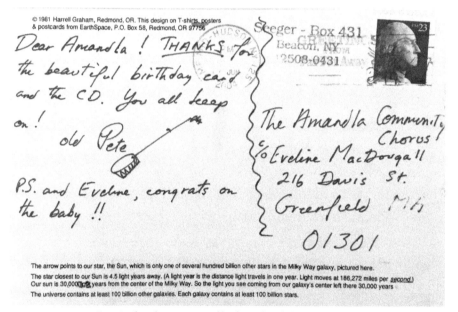

Pete's thanks to Amandla for a birthday card with
congratulations to Eveline on the birth of Gillis

It could've been a lullabye

Plattsburgh, New York, where I spent much of my childhood, is not far from the largest maximum-security prison in the state. Locals refer to the Clinton Correctional Facility as Dannemora after the village where it's situated.

The name evokes loathing in people of all ages. I recall slumber party storytelling sessions about infamous throat slitters, violent rapists, and serial killers housed at Dannemora. I remember trying to sleep after hearing such tales, knowing that hundreds of unrepentant, hardened criminals just thirteen miles away hatched devious plans for escape while we lay in our sleeping bags.

In 1978, at age fourteen, I glimpsed another side of Dannemora. I volunteered each Saturday morning at five o'clock in a church basement where brown-skinned women and children from New York City stopped in Plattsburgh on their way to visit loved ones locked up in Dannemora.

The chaos and heartbreak of my volunteer shifts made a deep impression. My first real peek into the US justice system was of weary mothers and grandmothers with numb, exhausted children in tow. They boarded the bus in New York City around midnight and tumbled out, pre-dawn, blinking in disbelief at our quiet little town.

My responsibilities included handing out disposable diapers, making sure doughnuts, juice, and coffee didn't run out, and keeping the hectic bathrooms stocked with paper goods.

The project started when my friend's dad felt inspired to establish a pit stop in the basement of his church after learning that prisoners' loved ones arrived at the forbidding institution disheveled and hungry, desperate for a chance to see family members. Recognizing that he couldn't singlehandedly fix the gargantuan problems of racism and oppression in our criminal justice system, still he wanted to do something.

Welcoming the tired travelers left me wondering what it would be like to have everything stacked against me. Given my large, fun-loving family, I couldn't imagine visits happening rarely, briefly, and behind thirty-foot walls.

I learned about injustice from my parents and in my church but had not learned the most terrible truths about these United States. In meeting those women and their sleepy children, I didn't yet know that the architects of South African apartheid used American Jim Crow laws as a blueprint for their inhumane system. I had no clue that, despite abbreviated, heroic depictions of the civil rights era shown on filmstrips in school, Jim Crow still pervaded our nation.

I visited the village of Dannemora for the first time at the age of sixteen to spend time with a school chum. I found a closed society largely made up of the institution, prison workers, and their families. Given time, I might have discovered more depth, but to my teen-aged sensibilities in 1980, it was just as I'd imagined as a child.

A decade later, while planning an Amandla/Barwa tour through upstate New York and Vermont, I acted on a suggestion from the Reverend Jack Studebaker of the Newman Center at the State University of New York at Plattsburgh. Jack loved the thought of social-justice songs performed at the maximum-security lock-up.

It would be Amandla's first prison gig. Before starting Amandla, I had sung at minimum- and medium-security prisons with the Noonday Singers, but neither the singers nor I had sung at a maximum-security institution.

The Amandla/Barwa tour came one year after we met one of the most famous prisoners of all time soon after his release from nearly thirty years in South African prisons. Accounts of Nelson Mandela's imprisonment revealed to me that life is far more complex than "bad guys get arrested and go to jail, making society safer." That narrative is readily available in popular culture, but reading Mandela's essays and those of other activist prisoners exposed me to a broader view of so-called criminal justice systems.

Navigating loads of red tape, I received permission to perform at Dannemora. I couldn't decide whether it was a dream come true or a potential nightmare.

Still sleepy on a Saturday morning after a boisterous, standing-room-only show at Plattsburgh State the night before, the singers headed west to the facility. They looked bleary after precious few hours in guest bedrooms and on living room floors provided by host families.

I worked hard to secure approval to do the show, but once we actually traveled toward the prison on that warm morning, the thought of passing beyond thick walls and being locked in, even as performers with permission to leave, left me shivering.

New York's Route 374 travels within yards of the thirty-foot southern perimeter wall. The prison looked even more massive than I remembered. I saw expressions of concern on singers' faces as the fortress came into view. I tried to appear calm as we approached the facility with three thousand prisoners and one thousand guards, but my heart pounded.

We filed through an entrance where grim-faced correctional officers escorted us down a hallway. Each door opened with a loud buzz and shut with a deafening clang. There's nothing like traveling deep into the bowels of a huge prison to trigger claustrophobia. I wonder how guards and prisoners can stand it day after day.

Three years into my work as a choral director, I had learned a few things about leading a singing group. But it wasn't until that day that I understood the importance of setting the tone in stressful situations. I tried to appear calm while walking through prison hallways, but I was scared, and my mouth was completely dry.

It took a while for forty singers to go through metal detectors and get patted down. As we approached the door to the gymnasium where the performance would take place, an administrator sternly advised us about the consequences of breaking any rules. The tiniest infraction would result in immediate suspension of the show. He repeated a long list of regulations we'd already memorized.

His final words before we entered the gym: "Remember, of all the rules, the two most important are 'Don't cross the line,' and 'Don't touch a prisoner in any way.' If any one of you makes physical contact with a prisoner, the show is over and you're in big trouble. Understand?"

I nodded, but he repeated the word until I said it, too. "I understand," I said. "We all understand." Singers nodded.

In the middle of the gym stood a plain but sturdy stage. Forty pairs of feet ascended rough-sawn steps. From the stage, we saw wide yellow tape on the floor and recognized the demarcation as the line we mustn't cross.

Several yards beyond the line were two hundred metal folding chairs in rows with a wide aisle separating two sections. The set-up did not create a cozy feeling.

A door opened. Twelve guards stepped in and formed a gauntlet through which each prisoner passed. The men in prison garb walked with a variety of gaits. Some were loose, rhythmic, and jaunty, while others advanced stiffly. On the whole, the men seemed young, but there were some older guys, too. I saw men who looked strong and vibrant, while others struck me as cautious and overly alert. I saw scars. Many displayed tattoos.

Within moments, I noticed in the stream of humanity moving toward the chairs that nearly every man had brown skin. Men looking beautiful or dull, enthusiastic or bored, anticipatory or sleepy: they filed in until the chairs were filled.

These are the men of the harried women and sleepy children, I realized, . . . *the women and children I met when I was fourteen while volunteering at the stopover for prisoners' families.* I scanned the men's faces and wondered who among them received visitors and who felt forgotten. *Some of these guys have loved ones who ride through the night on buses in order to visit them in this godforsaken place,* I thought.

Someone cleared a throat, and I noticed guards positioned around the perimeter. *Oh, I'm supposed to start the show.*

Putting on a smile, I stepped to the microphone. Before I could say a word, though, I heard a gasp from behind me. I turned to see one of our South African friends, a man who'd been imprisoned for political activity in his country. His face was frozen in disbelief as he looked out over the familiar sight of dark-skinned men in prison.

He shook his head slowly as if under water. His lips, a thin line, parted when he emitted an anguished sound. He headed toward the stairs, and I made a small gesture. As he descended the steps, I made no movement. I watched his feet land on the floor and travel toward the men. The air seemed deadly still. We watched, bewildered, as our friend crossed The Line.

The men in chairs didn't move a muscle. Some tried to follow the singer's movements with their eyes but didn't turn their heads as he walked by. The guards' hands, in unison, raised dark objects, but I refused to focus my eyes on them because I didn't want to know whether the objects were rifles or batons. I had no idea what to do.

Our friend walked all the way down the wide aisle, stopping only when he reached the far wall. He rested his forehead on the wall, his body wracked by muffled sobs. Slowly, the seated men turned to look. Making no sudden moves, they shifted almost imperceptibly until every man could survey the scene. The sobs continued, and there was no other movement.

Someone will do something, I thought, *but what? Am I supposed to do something?*

Then, a soft voice called, "C'mon back, Bro, iss aw-right."

Others echoed: "Iss aw-right, yeah."

"You aw-right now. You come back, Brotha."

Voices joined in until two hundred men murmured in tones so soothing, it could've been a lullabye: "Iss aw-right, good Brotha, you be aw-right. "

Guards remained rigidly poised. Prisoners continued calling to their South African brother until their humming message of love reached him. He lifted his forehead from the wall, turned, and took in the group of human beings calling to him with everything they had.

Tears soaked the front of his shirt. He looked utterly drained, yet with a deep, shuddering sigh, he took one step and began the long, slow walk back to the stage. A grin spread over his damp face as prisoners clapped in unison with each step he took. Knowing full well that they were forbidden to stand, the men lifted a few inches off their chairs to express solidarity.

When his foot hit the stage, I grabbed our friend's hand and whispered, "You OK?" He nodded. As he stepped into the chorus, he was steadied and welcomed by many hands.

The guards lowered their dark objects and remained in position. No one marched to the stage to cancel the show, so I stepped to the microphone and said, "Gentlemen, we're going to sing."

I heard loud requests: "Put the brothers and sisters up front!" I saw the South African singers standing in the very back row. I invited them to step out front. They did, hesitant at first. Then they waved and grinned.

The prisoners cheered. I couldn't hear my pitch pipe over the din, but it didn't matter. By some miracle, the unforgettable show went on.

Singers from Barwa and Amandla ride the ferry to Burlington, Vermont following the April, 1991, high-intensity performance at Clinton Correctional Facility, New York State's largest maximum-security prison.

This time, he meets my gaze

Twenty-four men — most of them brown-skinned — made up the audience as Amandla performed the first of two shows at the Franklin County Jail in November of 2000. The men were shy at first but warmed quickly. Many awaited deportation hearings due to trouble with the what was then known as the Immigration and Naturalization Service (INS) following a ruling that put foreign prisoners in the hot seat.

They responded to my request by calling out names of their homelands: Jamaica, Haiti, Trinidad and Tobago, Dominican Republic, Cambodia, Vietnam, Guinea, Ghana. One sad-looking fellow said in a rumbling voice, "Sout' Africa."

One tall, very dark-skinned man with a greying beard closed his eyes and swayed during the spirituals, adding counterpoint.

A Haitian fellow accepted my invitation when I asked, "Would anyone like to share a song from your country?" He sang about the pain of separation from God.

I was sorry to see the sweet and responsive group go when the half hour was up, and they made it clear they wished they could stay. I shook the hand of Bradley, whom I'd met before. As they filed out, the Haitian man gave me a nice hug. We had about two minutes to prepare for the next group: prisoners wearing orange jumpsuits to signify that they awaited sentencing.

The men in the second group looked younger than the others, and more sullen. As they filed in, I knew this show could be a letdown after the warmth of the previous one. The young guys sat along the wall, hesitant to be part of an audience. There were a few neutral faces, but most seemed closed. One guy way in the back looked deeply depressed and very skinny, with long unkempt hair and bags under his eyes.

I worked much harder than during the previous show. I coasted on faith that songs, lovingly offered, are never lost. A few small smiles formed, and some guys nodded. Eventually, a few even sang along. I was delighted when a Cuban fellow agreed to read a few lines in Spanish from a poem about peace.

I recited Ina Hughes's "Prayer for Responsibility for Children," and we followed up with the soothing "Circle Round for Freedom" by Linda Hirschhorn. The Amandla singers looked gentle and kind.

As we wrapped up, I asked, "Does anyone have a song or a poem they'd like to share?" This time, however, my invitation was met with stony silence. We ended with the upbeat "Dios Donde Quiera Esta," a Central American song about community and faith.

The men left, and the singers moved through the jail toward the exit. An administrator approached, smiling. "One of the men went to get a poem for you." She added, "You made quite an impact tonight."

I tried to imagine which prisoner would return with a poem. The kind-faced man who sat to my right? The Cuban? As we waited, we sang "Freedom Is Coming" in an open central area where we could see men pressed against two tiers of bars.

"Here he comes," the administrator said. I was stunned. It was the skinny guy with tired eyes. Shyly, he handed me a sheet of paper.

"I wrote this for my daughter," he said. The title, written in block letters, was "Time for All My Sins." Underneath was written "By Enrique."

I looked at him in wonder.

He said, "I want you to have it. I have another copy in my cell."

"Thank you very much, Enrique," I said, taking his hand. "As you could tell from the show, I love poetry." The men watching us through the bars fell silent for the first time since we arrived. All eyes were on us. The poet shifted uncomfortably.

"May I share this with my singers?" I asked.

Enrique's eyes widened. I recognized a man accustomed to asking for permission, not granting it. He nodded.

"This is a beautiful gift," I said quietly.

He looked away and said flatly, "Yeah."

I put my hand on his arm. "Enrique, I mean it. This is a beautiful gift."

This time, he met my gaze. His eyes became moist. He nodded, looked down, and whispered, "Yeah."

He walked back to where people lived, thought, and slept surrounded by bars and locks. My singers started "Freedom Is Coming" again, and we walked to the exit.

In the parking lot, we saw that some of the men peered through barred windows to wave good-bye. I pondered concepts of sin and crime. I thought about what it means to take drugs and be desperate for more. I wondered what it feels like to hit bottom and steal money, a TV set, a car. To sell one's body, or to destroy that of another.

I don't romanticize prisoners. Several close friends have lost family members to violent crime. Survivors experience devastating, incalculable, and irreversible loss at the hands of desparate individuals. Make no mistake: some prisoners scare, sadden, or fill me with rage.

Yet still I wonder: what does it mean to poison a river, denude a forest, or drop bombs on civilians? I detest knowing that money is allotted for shiny new missiles while children go without schoolbooks. Dealmakers attend elegant dinners while children go without breakfast. Yet when some of these children grow up to commit dangerous acts, we fail to see the connection.

Leaving the jail that night, I glanced once more at the locked-up men and recognized them as question marks punctuating our culture. Where were the children of financiers and politicians? Did they never break rules? Where were the crooked bankers? Why are our prison audiences always made up of the poorest, darkest, or forsaken?

I have not lived a perfect life. Yet every time I sing or teach at a prison, I finish the program and the gate shuts behind me with a clang.

I am free to go.

We presented two shows in the library of the Franklin County lock-up. The first concert included many Immigration and Naturalization Service (INS) prisoners from our appearance a few weeks earlier. They sang along enthusiastically.

Six young, white, edgy fellows awaiting sentencing comprised the next group. It was tough going. After each song, they clapped awkwardly, sheepishly peeking at each other. We made a nice connection toward the end, however, with "Ipharadisi," a South African song honoring loved ones who have passed from this world.

Aware that my invitation could fall flat, I encouraged the men to share names of loved ones they'd lost. They surprised me by participating, each one, some adding vignettes about grandparents, an uncle, a dog.

The sweetness of humanity often lies just beneath the surface, I mused, *even when a person seems shut down.*

The men clapped enthusiastically when we finished the show. Singers bade them farewell with handshakes and hugs.

A guard came to collect our audience. The singers prepared to leave, but I said, "It's been such a positive evening, I'm tempted to ask if there are others we can sing for briefly before we leave. Maybe a few women downstairs in the tiny unit?" Singers nodded, indicating that they, too, were in no hurry to head home.

I conferred with a guard, who picked up a phone. His face betrayed no emotion as he relayed my offer to an administrator.

Hanging up, he said, "You can do twenty minutes in the SU." His face twitched. Amusement? Disgust? I couldn't tell.

"The SU?" I asked, unfamiliar with the term.

"Segregated Unit," he said curtly. "Men who can't be in the general population. If you really want to sing there, you got twenty minutes, starting now."

He made a face as though he'd stepped in dog poop. Narrowing his eyes, he shook his head slowly from side to side as if thinking, *You're an idiot, and your stupid project stinks.*

"Thank you," I said. "For us, it's a gift to share our songs without judgment." I tried to connect with him, but his expression remained unchanged.

Hastily informing the singers, I said, "I've never been to this unit, so I can't tell you what to expect. Just stick together, please."

I was struck by the low ceiling and isolated feeling of the SU with men kept singly in eight windowless cells in a row, facing a blank wall. The dimly lit area felt like a cave or something from another century.

Yet given the unit's name, there was more leeway than I anticipated: at the end of the cramped unit, four men sat at a small table outside the cells. They played chess or leafed through magazines. Two men remained locked in while two others sat in cells with doors wide open. There were no guards — known as COs or correctional officers — in the space, but I could see one near the entrance to what I'd come to think of as The Cave.

Taking stock of the layout, I suggested to the singers that they fan out to create the possibility for each prisoner to look into the eyes of an Amandla member if he desired.

The unusual layout made for challenging acoustics. The ceiling was so low that our tallest singer (6'6") was unable to stand up straight. I paced the length of the unit while nodding and smiling to each man, and directed the first couple of songs.

A young Vietnamese fellow locked in his cell responded hungrily to news that we knew a song from his country. "Which song?" he asked in a tone that betrayed disbelief.

I hummed the opening phrase, and he exclaimed, "I know that song!" Chorus members began to relax, finally peeling themselves from the wall and stepping forward to sing to the young fellow who pressed his face between the bars.

We sang about young lovers meeting in secret on a bridge, hiding news of their love from their parents until the very end of the song. When I first heard James Durst sing the haunting melody, I wanted to arrange it for chorus. It took me ten years to come up with a version I liked.

When we arrived, most of the men looked blank and bored, but the Vietnamese prisoner's eyes, mouth, and expression were wide open. When we finished, he closed his eyes and slumped down several inches but with hands in the same high position, clutching the bars, as when he'd stood upright.

"I thank . . . " he whispered. "I thank you." Opening his eyes, he asked in a quiet voice, "How? How do you know it?"

I smiled. "It's a long story. I heard a friend sing it and knew I wanted to learn it." I took a breath and said what was in my heart: "Now I understand why I wanted to sing it. I hope we've brought you a few moments of peace."

His hands slid down the bars. He backed away and sat on his bunk, hugging his knees, head down. He glanced up and nodded.

An angry man, three cells down, launched into a tirade in heavily accented English, using phrases like, "Dumped in here . . . big mistake . . . this shithole . . . "

I knew we could not fully hear and honor the Russian man's story in our short time but wasn't sure how to cut him off.

"Sir," I said, flustered, "I wish we had time to hear your whole story, but we have just a few minutes. We're here to share songs in the hope that . . . "

Dejected, he turned away. I grabbed the arm of Gary, a longtime Amandla member. "Sir, this is Gary. His family comes from Russia." Gary said a couple of phrases in Russian. The prisoner's countenance changed as he leaned forward and spoke rapidly.

Gary replied in Russian that he didn't understand a great deal of the language, just basic phrases. It didn't matter. The angry man stood up straighter, looking energized. The two exchanged a few more phrases and, this time, the man behind bars spoke more slowly and lowered his voice.

Gary shook the man's hand. I said, "We'll end with a lullabye called 'Dreams of Harmony.' It says goodnight in nine languages, including Russian."

I remarked to the Russian fellow, "Please be patient with us. We've struggled with the Russian pronunciation, even with Gary's help."

The man raised an eyebrow and said, "Do-bray no-chi?"

Confused, I said. "No, it's something else?"

Gary stepped forward to explain. "This song uses 'Spokoynyye nochi.'"

"Oh!' the man said, repeating the phrase twice, making it sound like water flowing over rocks. "You find this dee-fi-cult?!" He laughed heartily.

I beckoned the singers to gather in front of his cell. "This fellow really knows how to say it," I said. "Maybe he can help us." He grew shy but looked pleased. I requested, "Would you do us a favor? Will you say 'good night' so my singers can hear how it's really done?"

He drew himself up to his full height with a flourish and said, using a dramatic 1930s horror movie voice: "Gooooood Niiiiiiight!" Everyone in the unit cracked up.

"No!" I protested. "In Russian!"

Chuckling, he said, "Oh, Russian? That easy language?" He said the beautiful phrase several times, gesturing that we should try it. Shaking his head, he drilled us until satisfied. "Not perfect," he admitted, "but I understand what you say."

Asking singers to fan out once more, we sang the beautiful song by Joanne Olshansky. As the last note faded, I stepped to the bars and reached for our tutor. He grasped my hands as I thanked him in Russian, "Spa-see-bah," a word I recalled from two semesters of Russian language study. Squeezing my hands gently, he repeated the word.

I'm from Nigeria, too!

Sam Abiloye, a talented musician with a deep belly laugh and great stories, informed us at rehearsal one evening that he would soon move back to Nigeria to be with family. Chorus members groaned when we heard the news but cheered ourselves up by planning a fantastic going-away party.

We gathered at the Amherst organic farm where Sam lived and worked. We reminisced, feasted (making sure to sample Sam's delicious fried plantains), danced, sang, and showered our friend with good wishes and gifts.

As the party wound down, I asked Sam, "Is there a song we haven't sung this evening that you'll miss?"

Sam nodded. "Yah, I love that Hebrew one. The one about faith — that's my favorite."

The singers gathered, our arms around each other in a big circle. "Ani Ma'Amin" is an excerpt from a twelfth-century prayer written by Moses ben Maimonides. Later set to music, it expresses faith in the coming of the Messiah. Maimonides was a gifted healer, scholar, and community leader.

Jewish Partisans sang the ancient prayer during World War II. People sang it in the Warsaw Ghetto and in boxcars headed to concentration camps. I learned "Ani Ma'Amin" from Jim Levinson at Noonday Farm. Jim explained, "In the face of horror, the prayer offers majestic affirmation of hope: 'Even though the Messiah tarries, still I believe.'"

We sang the rich harmonies for several minutes, then remained in silence. A friend later said, "I could've stayed in that circle for hours. We didn't really want to say goodbye to Sam."

The time came, however, to gather empty potluck dishes and get in line to give Sam "one more hug, one more hug." I headed to the parking lot with carpool buddies, remembering when Sam made a huge difference at an event where the Amandla Chorus was booed for the first and only time.

When I received an invitation to sing at an Enfield, Connecticut, prison in honor of Black History Month, I thought of our many brown-skinned brothers and sisters locked up across the US. Painfully aware of the roles racism and white privilege play in our national tragedy, I always emphasize that—while Amandla sometimes has African or African-American members— the chorus has many members who are of European ancestry. I've learned the importance of asking about needs and expectations of groups who invite us to perform.

Unbeknownst to me, the Enfield invitation originated with someone who had dishonorable intentions. I don't have all the facts, but I do know that the prisoner who claimed to represent the Black History Month committee tossed the promotional photo I sent. Instead, he posted a photo of a Black African group, something I didn't learn until days later. Upon arriving at the facility, I met the so-called committee member and saw that his skin color matched my own.

I'll never forget what happened next.

When we arrived to sing, we caused a stir among 250 men sitting on gymnasium bleachers. Led to believe the show would feature an African group, tensions rose quickly among the men. Amandla singers, very few of them of African descent, tried to remain calm despite the cacophony of boos increasing in volume.

The experience taught me the value of being booed at least once in a lifetime. Applause is easy to take, whether it's earnest or polite. Being booed, however, shook my core and forced me to ask myself, *Who am I? Why am I here?* It was an important moment of reckoning.

A brown-skinned prisoner in charge of running the sound system shifted the energy by stepping to the microphone. "Brothers, I'm ashamed of your actions. These people are here to bring us joy. It's not their fault that someone," he paused, "*Someone* misrepresented them on the poster! Please give them your respect and attention! How would you want to be treated?"

I believe the song "On Children" also helped ease the difficult situation. Ysaye Barnwell of Sweet Honey in the Rock set Khalil Gibran's words to music and created a brilliant work of art. We dedicated the song to the prisoners' children. Many years later, Karen, an Amandla singer from southern Vermont, recalled: "I'll never forget how the men changed from sounding angry to looking very sad. Many bowed their heads as we sang in honor of their children, and I saw many tears."

I often wonder, *Who am I to bring freedom songs into prisons, especially when white privilege is at the root of mass incarceration?* Yet I'm convinced by connections we make with incarcerated people that the work is important and that I always have a lot to learn.

The men in the audience called out, "Let's hear the brother play the drum!" Sam, holding his djembe, grinned and waved.

I invited Sam to the microphone and introduced him as an Amandla member from Nigeria.

A man in the first row rocketed from his bleachers seat and slapped a hand to his chest. "I'm from Nigeria!"

Sam said loudly, "I am from Lagos."

The Nigerian prisoner exclaimed, "I'm from Lagos!"

Many prisoners and Amandla singers laughed.

Sam asked, "Do you know 'Oni Dodo'?"

The man jumped up and down. "I'm from Nigeria, man! Of course I know 'Oni Dodo'!!"

"Come sing it with me, Brother!" crowed Sam. The audience applauded thunderously and stomped their feet.

Some Amandla members knew the iconic song about fried plantains sold to a hungry crowd in a marketplace. We joined in as the two men sang into the microphone while Sam played the djembe.

Prison staff made no move to prevent the prisoner from crossing the line on the floor. As the two Nigerians sang, the line seemed to disappear, along with walls, bleachers, and prison garb.

The song ended, and the two men embraced tightly for what seemed like a long time. The gym, previously filled with boos, filled with cheers and laughter. We wrapped up the show to a standing ovation. Men called out, "Don't go! Come back soon! Thank you!"

I am astounded, every time: the power of song, the power of love.

Working mom

Given my employment profile and wage-earning history, I do not have standard forms of security or benefits. Yet I enjoy the flexibility of the gig economy and being my own boss.

Until I read the phrase "gig economy" in *Yes!* magazine, I did not know that my way of life possesses such a hip descriptor. *Ah ha*, I thought. *There's a name for what I do.*

Choral director, editor, fiddler, housecleaner, substitute teacher . . . even into my fifties, I make and take work where I can while seeking meaning and worthwhile commitment.

One thing I love about being self-employed is that my boss doesn't protest when I take my kid to work with me. Though

Eveline and Gillis relax between sound check and performance, 2010.

not an official member of our chorus, Gillis participates in some programs and encounters fascinating people and songs along the way.

It's not wall-to-wall excitement, to be sure. Events sometimes include cooling our heels between an early sound check and the start of an event. We anticipate lulls by packing books or an UNO deck. Down time occurs fairly rarely in the performing arts, though, and Gillis began roadie work at an early age, especially after Douglas

Eveline and Douglas Reid perform as Fire Pond.

and I formed our musical duo, Fire Pond. As roadie, Gillis hauls props, sound equipment, and boxes of concert programs. Gillis is no stranger to the assignment.

I cherish moments with Gillis surrounded by community arts. At five, he waited patiently at a local farm festival. He knew that when Mama finished singing, he would sit on a tractor, hands on the steering wheel as he made "R-r-r-u-m, R-r-r-u-m" sounds.

At age six, Gillis joined participants of all ages at a celebration of languages sponsored by the Greenfield Public Library. He belted out lyrics in seven different languages that evening.

Following the death of Nelson Mandela in 2013, Gillis slipped into the chorus when, taking up songs he's heard all his life, Amandla hosted a commemorative open sing. A pack of tenors leaned in around Gillis during the "Freedom Is Coming" descant.

Gillis entered the world already familiar with Amandla's repertoire, since he heard them frequently while in utero. When my labor began, four dear Amandla singers graced our home with freedom songs, soothing my contractions.

Gillis in the tenor section at Amandla's tribute to Nelson Mandela in January, 2014, a few weeks after Mandela's death.
Joan Featherman, Lisa Finestone, Betsy Evans, and Wisty Rorabacher welcome him, from left, in Greenfield's Temple Israel.

Gillis soaked up music differently than I did as a child. Rooted in symphony halls, my experiences featured woodwinds, brass, strings, percussion, tuxedos, and music representing the eighteenth and nineteenth centuries from a few dominant countries.

In contrast, my son grew up immersed in music from all over the world and spanning more than seven centuries. He heard songs celebrating women, children, workers, farmers, activists, heroes, and anonymous people from all walks of life. My childhood soundtrack represented narrow slices of culture, gender, and geography, but Gillis acquired wider tastes and understood more about world culture and arts at five than I did at fifteen.

Gillis's musical education, often transmitted on the fly, did not stop at Amandla's repertoire. With access to dozens of musical instruments at home, Gillis explored early and often. Before he turned one, he liked to occupy my accordion box any time I pulled the instrument out.

Playing a sprightly tune, I sat on the floor in my pajamas one day. Gillis climbed out of the accordion box and toddled over to his small hand drum. When I completed a phrase, he added a wild drum break complete with primal yell. To this day, we sometimes punctuate moments of exultation by yelling, "Drum break!"

Gillis and I traveled to schools and day care centers to facilitate children putting their hands on a wide variety of musical instruments. Priceless facial expressions occur when a three- or four-year-old draws a bow across cello strings, strikes a marimba, or hypnotically turns a rain stick over and over.

At the Giving Tree School in Gill one afternoon, I played zampoña, a traditional Andean instrument, while adding marimba

counterpoint. When I finished, questions poured from small children's mouths. Gillis formulated a reply more quickly than I to satisfy an inquiry from one of his peers: "It's called a zampoña," he said, "but you can also call it pan pipes. When you play it, you blow through a little smile."

Gillis lets it rip as he jams with Mom in 2005.

Noticing a busker in front of our food co-op, seven-year-old Gillis asked, "Why is there money in his guitar case?"

"People who enjoy his music show appreciation by sharing some of their money," I told him.

"What does he do with the money?" Gillis asked. "Does he buy guitar strings?"

"He might," I replied. "Or maybe he buys cheese or pays the phone bill." I told Gillis that I once earned enough money busking in New Orleans to buy a plane ticket back to Massachusetts. I did not tell him of being chased by a cop on horseback due to my repeated offense of busking in that city without a permit. "I've enjoyed playing music on the streets of many cities and towns," I added. "Memphis, Albuquerque, even Greenfield."

"When?" he demanded.

"Before you were born."

He considered this news before making a proposal: "Can we?"

"Can we what, Honey?" I asked, prompting him to flesh out his plan.

Eveline and Gillis perform for kids at the Giving Tree School in Gill, Massachusetts in 2009.

"Can we play tunes in front of the co-op and leave our cases open, like him?" he asked, pointing toward the musician who moved to pack up.

"Well-l-l-l-l . . ." I said hesitantly, "What would we play?"

"You on fiddle, me on guitar," he responded confidently. "We know 'Angeline, the Baker' and 'Whiskey before Breakfast.'"

"I've never busked with just two tunes," I mused. "I'll tell you what: if it's sunny tomorrow and if you promise to practice with me at home first, we'll give it a try. I'm pretty sure we can fit you and both instruments in the bike cart." Gillis was accustomed to making plans while taking into account the fact that I didn't own a car.

The next day dawned clear. We set up in front of the co-op and played two tunes for about ten minutes, earning twelve

Eveline and Gillis busk at the co-op in 2009.

dollars. Feeling flush, we bought a sandwich, an avocado, and one freshly made éclair. We sat outside to guard our instruments while smearing our fingers and faces with chocolate and custard. I can't imagine a happier duo.

Gillis remained at home with Papa while I went off to certain kinds of engagements. He usually accepted it with grace, but at six years old, he registered displeasure as I dressed for a Green River String Band wedding gig.

"Why are you wearing a fancy dress, Mama?" he pouted.

"You know why, Sweetheart. The band is playing at a wedding, so the guys and I need to wear nice clothes."

"I have nice clothes," he retorted, pulling train-engineer coveralls from a drawer.

"You certainly do," I agreed, "and you look especially nice in your coveralls. But you still have to stay with Papa today."

Gillis pursed his lips and revealed the true source of his unhappiness. "I bet they'll have cake."

"Yo ho, so that's it!" I teased. "You don't want to hear Mama's band. You want cake!"

He ran outside, erupting in giggles. I chased him around the side yard.

"Cake is good!" he yelled.

"I'm wearing fancy shoes and can't run as fast as you!" I shouted my weak excuse.

He hid behind the big butternut tree and peeked at me from one side. "You never run as fast as me," he taunted, sticking out his tongue.

"Ha!" I said, for want of a brilliant rejoinder. "Wait until I put my sneakers on later. Also, later, you may find a piece of wedding cake wrapped in a pretty party napkin." Narrowing my eyes, I added, "Play your cards right."

Changing his tune, Gillis asked, "Can I help you load the bike cart, Mama?"

He knew my plan to transport fiddle, viola, accordion, and my microphones by pedal power. We managed to pack it all in. I neglected to factor, however, the reality of cycling across town in fancy clothes. A safety pin transformed my dress into modest culottes, and away I went.

Mollified by the prospect of cake, Gillis bade me farewell but couldn't resist sticking out his tongue in one last defiant gesture before I pushed off.

Gillis couldn't resist sticking out his tongue in one last defiant gesture.

Wally and Juanita Nelson

I met Wally and Juanita Nelson in 1986, soon after my father died. I was twenty-one. The Nelsons' forthright wisdom and courage inspired me. Over many years, our mutual affection grew until I considered them my second set of parents. During my twenties and thirties, I lived with them in Deerfield, Massachusetts, several times.

Toward the ends of their lives, the Nelsons lived in my Greenfield home for stretches of time. Wally died in the bedroom where, two years later, I labored for thirty hours as baby Gillis Nelson Thompson MacDougall prepared to make his entry.

For many years, the Nelsons grew produce in their large garden, called The Bean Patch, to sell at the Greenfield Farmer's Market and local eateries. Their hand-built cabin sat on land owned by the Woolman Hill Quaker Retreat Center.

Wally and Juanita shared stories from their early days in the civil rights movement, pre-dating the activism of Rosa Parks and Dr. King. Listening to their stories, I heard songs in my mind: "Oh, freedom. Oh, freedom. Oh, freedom over me."

A decade after we met, the Nelsons began collaborating with Amandla, weaving freedom songs with civil rights stories as well as vignettes about right livelihood. Their stories mesmerized audiences of all ages. Our shared projects deepened my bonds with Wally and Juanita.

Lifelong activists, the Nelsons devoted their last several decades to authentic democracy that took into account the health of soil, air, and water. But it might not have been so. Their early experiences nudged them away from farming as they grew up in African-American families stressed by poisonous injustice.

Wally and Juanita on a 1950s outing with friends

Born in rural Arkansas in 1909, Wally noted at the age of six that his family's sharecropping work bore a striking resemblance to the slavery that battered and scarred his ancestors. The experience soured Wally on farm work. He wanted to make an honest living while wearing a clean suit, dress shoes, and a dapper hat, a goal he reached after graduating from high school at the age of twenty-one.

The eleventh of twelve children, Wally found it necessary to take time off from school now and again to earn money to buy books and shoes. He and his younger brother Merrill persevered until they each earned diplomas.

Wally and Juanita met while he was in jail for refusing to fight in World War II. Not only did he consider it absurd to fight on behalf of a nation that did not ensure his basic human rights, but Wally also, in principle, considered fighting in all forms to be wrong. So Wally took his resistance a step further, walking out of a camp for conscientious objectors after realizing he did not want to do any work for the war effort, even in a CO camp.

Visiting the jail as a reporter for the Cleveland *Call and Post*, Juanita investigated a story about segregated conditions in the jail where Wally awaited trial. He was sentenced to three years. The couple got together after his release. They each took a series of paying jobs while volunteering many hours in the early civil rights movements.

Juanita, a city girl, had no wish to get her hands dirty. Her parents participated in the Great Migration to northern cities where Blacks found jobs and a measure of increased security, though by no means guaranteed.

Her family settled in Cleveland and referred in somber tones to the aunt who was lynched by a Georgia mob enraged by a strong Black woman standing up to racism. The first in her family to attend college, Juanita worked as a journalist and, later, a speech therapist. "Every day I went to work dressed to the nines," Juanita loved to say.

Wally's longest employment stint, with the Antioch Bookplate Company, allowed him to work as a sub-contractor and enabled him to avoid having taxes withheld. A real estate bargain led the Nelsons to purchase a large home in Philadelphia, where they hosted many meetings of activists and resisters.

In midlife, however, the Nelsons yearned for increased self-sufficiency and fewer ties with oppressive systems. Surprising even herself, Juanita suggested they consider farming.

Wally recoiled at the suggestion and reminded Nita: "For people with beautiful brown skin, farming resembles slavery."

Juanita countered with an observation: "The people who seem most free are those who work the land, providing for their own basic needs."

Not for the first time, Juanita won Wally over with her reasoning. The Nelsons embarked on the rhythms, heartbreaks, and triumphs of farming.

A significant shift occurred in the late 1960s. The Nelsons sold their large Philadelphia home and rented a place in Ojo Caliente, New Mexico. With pointers from new friends, they grew enough produce in a large garden to feed themselves and to sell surplus at market. Juanita was convinced, and Wally came along with her. They wanted to stay in New Mexico, but their lease ended and they couldn't find an affordable piece of land.

At the behest of renowned antiwar activist Randy Kehler, the Woolman Hill Quaker Center in Deerfield invited Wally and Juanita (at sixty-five and fifty years of age, respectively) to live on and cultivate a parcel of land. In 1974, the center's board bestowed on the Nelsons a ninety-nine-year lease.

The Nelsons discovered that, instead of a bitter pill, working the land offered a kind of freedom that was out of reach of their enslaved ancestors.

Spirited children of the Great Migration, Wally and Juanita in their earlier years gravitated to conveniences and style that came with city life and gainful employment. Yet in middle age, when many people reach for more luxuries, they embraced life without running water, electricity, flush toilet, or telephone. They felt the best way to "walk their talk" was to unplug from an economic system built on oppression.

I loved living and farming with the Nelsons. While harvesting tomatoes, pulling witch grass from the onion patch, or bundling carrots for market, I recognized that our backgrounds were similar, yet profoundly different.

The granddaughter of hardscrabble, proud Québécois subsistence farmers, I've done a lot of farm work and gardening. The Nelsons were grandchildren of enslaved people forced to work the land under brutal conditions. Farming was woven into our histories and lives, yet in vastly different ways.

I found good company among folks who sought inspiration in the Nelsons. Wally and Juanita provided superb leadership in many areas, including land trusts, farmer's markets, economic justice, pacifism, and living as localvores, eating mostly local products long before the term was coined. A topic of particular passion involved resistance to taxation by the US government, dollars which largely fund wars and militarism. The Nelsons' renown grew over the years, and they welcomed visitors from around the world, touching thousands of lives simply by living their ideals.

In 1996, Wally and Juanita joined Amandla onstage for the first of many concerts. My concerns about their waning physical strength led me to brainstorm about how they might earn income. At ages eighty-seven and seventy-three, they collected no social security nor any other benefits in order to stay clear of a federal government whose taxes they resisted. I saw that their days as subsistence farmers were numbered and they needed a new plan.

I pitched the idea to Amandla's steering committee, proposing that the Nelsons join our chorus on the concert circuit, with the caveat that a high percentage of payment go to Wally and Juanita. The committee unanimously supported my proposal.

The idea thrilled the Nelsons, who wanted to do real work in a way that required less heavy lifting and allowed for shorter hours in the fields.

We compiled lists of compatible stories and songs for performance, crafting a delightful collaboration.

Remarks by Wally at Deerfield Academy, 1999

Juanita and I were invited in 1957 to visit southwestern Georgia for four months to support a community called Koinonia [a Greek word meaning "fellowship"]. Koinonia was made up of people of many different skin shades living and working together, sharing everything communally. As you might guess, not everyone in Georgia thought that was a good idea at the time. To this day, misguided people continue to think it's not a good idea.

That year saw many incidents at Koinonia of gunshots fired from passing cars. Someone suggested a plan to provide a strong, peaceful presence at the community's entrance, in four-hour shifts. They asked Juanita and me to do shifts together.

Our job? To sit in a car out front of the community and remain calm. Easy to say, but harder to do in light of gunshots. Truth is, on our first shift, the first car came down the road, Nita and I hit the floor of the car and covered our heads, trembling. [He laughs.] So much for strong and peaceful! [Laughs even harder.]

We decided that instead of hitting the floor like a couple of cowards [spits out the word "cowards"], next time a car came along, we'd act differently. Throughout the rest of our shift, every time a car came down the road, we got out of the car and stood beneath a street lamp. This made us easy targets, but we decided we'd rather stand in the open and risk being shot than lose our dignity by cowering in the car.

The singers will now sing my favorite song . . .

Cue "Oh, Freedom."

Oh, freedom. Oh, freedom.
Oh, freedom over me. And before
I'd be a slave I'll be buried in my grave
And go home to my Lord and be free.

Later that evening, Wally grew tired and lost his train of thought. Stepping away from the microphone, he muttered and shook his head. Juanita's brow furrowed as Wally continued to search for words.

Wally saved the day by stepping to the microphone once more. To the students and staff, he said: "Nothing matters as long as I have this brilliant, beautiful companion by my side."

He pulled Juanita to him and planted a long kiss on her lips. The crowd went wild. Teenagers leapt to their feet in a long, standing ovation. I suspected it might be our last public presentation with Wally.

Indeed, it was.

I cued the singers for the last song. So ended our glorious collaborative performances with Wally Nelson.

Juanita's first arrest

The classroom of public middle school students, rural and mostly white, sat silently as Juanita told the story of her first arrest.

"My friend and I were students at Howard University in Washington, DC in the early 1940s. Sick and tired of segregation, we took matters into our own hands. Without much discussion, we walked into a downtown diner and ordered hot chocolate. The counter waitress said she wouldn't serve our kind. We told her our kind was human, just like her. We refused to move until we were served."

The Amandla singers stood off to the side as Nita told her story. I watched the kids more than I watched Nita, having heard her story dozens of times. While I never tired of hearing it, I loved watching students' reactions. Every single kid sat motionless.

"The waitress disappeared into the kitchen and came back with two mugs of hot chocolate filled only halfway. She slammed them down, spilling from each cup, and demanded twenty-five cents from each of us."

Juanita looked around the room, noting that the students hung on her every word.

"My friend and I pointed to the sign above our heads, which clearly stated that hot chocolate was a dime, not a quarter. The waitress answered quite rudely that, for us, the price was twenty-five cents. If we didn't pay, she would call the police."

Juanita paused, rubbing her hands together. I thought the students might burst from curiosity and suspense.

Finally, one bespectacled girl with two braids asked, "What did you do?"

Juanita smiled. "We did what was right. We each placed a dime on the counter and got up to leave. But as we turned around, two of DC's finest, police officers, told us we were under arrest for theft. They carted us off to jail."

The students sat, stunned. A few whispered to each other. Letting the story sink in, Juanita stood at the front of the classroom.

A freckled boy wearing a sports shirt raised his hand. "Mrs. Nelson, you were arrested even though you paid the price that was on the board? Even though you didn't get full cups of cocoa?" He shook his head, baffled.

Nita smiled. "Yes, my friend. That's correct. It doesn't make sense, does it? Oppression never makes sense."

A brown-skinned girl in a fuzzy purple sweater raised her hand and asked, "What happened at the jail?"

Nodding, Juanita replied, "We were put into a holding cell with several other women. Naïve, I was excited to be in jail for the first time. I hadn't thought the plan through but felt I was daring and brave. My friend and I talked with the other women and learned that most of them had been arrested for prostitution. Our conversations helped us see that these women were regular people like us, but were financially desperate.

"Those women had it tough," Juanita added somberly. "Their lives were very hard. When they asked me what it was like to go to college, I realized how lucky I was."

"How long were you in there?" asked a boy from the back row.

Juanita laughed. "Unfortunately, the dean of students came to get us out. She was angry with us, and we were disappointed that she interrupted our adventure, arriving just before lunch. In a way, though, her timing on that day contributed to my clean track record. Because I didn't get to eat lunch at the jail, I have a one hundred percent record of fasting while detained. Food has never passed my lips within the walls of a jail, even when I've been convicted and jailed for some weeks."

Her assertion caused another stir among the students. "How can you go weeks without food and not die?" cried a blond girl with a ponytail. "I can't stand when dinner is fifteen minutes late!"

This brought murmurs from the kids. Juanita waited until the commentary died down.

"You're kids," she pointed out. "You need regular nutrition. Every child in the world needs and deserves regular nutrition, and many don't get it. You probably know that, and it's a different story, although that story, too, is about oppression."

She went on. "Healthy adults can go without food for a while, especially if they stay hydrated. Sometimes I've fasted without water, too, which is much harder."

"WHY don't you eat food in jail?" asked a student, as many others nodded.

"Good question," said Nita. "When the government imprisons my body without my consent in response to my acts of conscience, I refuse to cooperate. If they punish me for standing up for my rights, they must take full responsibility for my life and upkeep. I won't make their job easier by capitulating to their violence."

Her words sank in and kids buzzed in quiet conversation, resuming discussion about how many meals they could skip and still survive.

"Remember," stressed Juanita, "it's a bad idea for children to skip meals. My choices to fast were made in adulthood when I faced hard decisions."

"How many times were you arrested?" asked a boy with dark curly hair.

"Lots of times!" Juanita replied. "Sometimes I intend to get arrested, other times it happens because I'm being myself. One time, Wally and I traveled home to Ohio from DC and stopped at a restaurant. We were very hungry, but they told us they didn't serve 'colored folks.' We sat at the table for a minute, trying to figure out what to do. The police arrived and carted us off to jail. They sent us to a mental institution for three weeks. That's another story altogether, and we're running out of time. If you're interested, I can tell you the happy ending of that one."

As one voice, the children cheered, "YES!" So Juanita continued.

"Due to an outpouring of support, we were released from the mental institution with charges dropped. The administration invited us back for a party. We were so happy to see both inmates and staff who became our friends while we were locked up there. Some of the nicest people we'd ever met threw us a wonderful party with cake and ice cream. Foolishly, Wally and I gorged ourselves. After three weeks without food, our stomachs weren't prepared for this feast, and we both got sick later. But it was so worth it!" She laughed.

Nita nodded at me, and I assembled the singers in the front of the classroom to sing, "We Shall Not Be Moved" followed by "Freedom Is Coming." We divided the class so they could participate in the call-and-response song.

When it was time to leave, the kids crowded around Juanita. She shook many hands. It seemed everyone wanted to touch her. One shy girl asked for Nita's autograph.

"I feel like a rock star!" laughed Juanita.

"You are a rock star," a tall boy replied. "You're a hero."

We must help

I dismissed rehearsal early. Twenty singers accompanied me to the hospital to sing for Wally. Many had shared the stage with him over several years. This time, we sang for a different reason.

His lips trembled as we began "Oh, Freedom." Tears slid from his eyes to the pillow.

Wally experienced precarious health as he neared ninety. I wondered how it would affect him to hear, "Before I'd be a slave, I'll be buried in my grave and go home to my Lord, and be free." Helpless in a hospital bed for a week, he endured a type of enslavement imposed by weakness. Tubes and needles kept him alive yet also acted as shackles.

The next verse, "No injustice," soothed Wally. When the song ended, he looked intently at each singer, then closed his eyes. "There are so many people being mistreated in this world," he said. "I'm crying, but not for myself. We must help people when they need us."

Moving words, but unsurprising statements coming from Wally. Guided by a fierce and loving quest for justice, Wally lived as simply as possible to limit his participation in oppressive systems. Though touched by Wally's words, I'd come to expect such sentiments from him.

When I visited Wally each day, I noticed an emaciated man covered in tattoos. He had no teeth. Hospital staff placed him next to the nurses' station. Strapped to a reclining chair due to agitation, he had stick-like legs.

Days earlier, I had asked a nurse, "Does he ever have visitors?"

She said, "Bruno? Never. That's partly why we keep him out here." I was astounded by the kindness shown by busy staff members at all hours.

After we finished our private concert for Wally, we left his room singing "Freedom Is Coming," bringing the song out into the hallway. With a swift motion, a nurse rolled Bruno over to us.

Bruno looked baffled by the sights and sounds of singers on the hospital ward. He gesticulated wildly with thin, papery hands. I crouched and put one hand on his arm and the other on his forehead as I did with Wally every day. Before that evening, I had barely registered Bruno as a person, even though I passed him in the hallway many times. He was merely the-old-guy-I-pass-while-rushing-to-Wally's-room. However, as I touched his arm and forehead, Bruno's sunken eyes pierced me, and I saw him as a person to be loved.

We must help people when they need us. Wally had said it moments before.

Bruno's eyes widened as singers gently patted and sang to him. He seemed to drink in each smile. His thin lips turned upward when we finished the song. He made sounds, but we couldn't understand a word.

A nurse whispered, "Pretend you're having a conversation." Bruno tipped his head this way and that, grunting and sighing.

To Bruno, I said, "Really? My goodness! I see..." and other small-talk phrases.

Gesturing and chuckling, Bruno grew more loquacious. He pointed to us. I asked, "Would you like to hear another song, Bruno?"

He nodded enthusiastically. He tried to clap as we sang a few more songs.

Finally, the singers headed home. I settled in at Wally's bedside, knowing that someone would relieve me at midnight. Community members maintained a schedule so Wally never had to be alone while in the hospital.

A nurse checked Wally's IV. She worked efficiently and did not look at me. She paused at the doorway, however, and returned to stand before me. "That's the best thing that's happened to Bruno since he arrived. Thank you. It was beautiful." She sped from the room.

I put one hand on Wally's arm and another on his brow. *Thank you, Wally. Thank you for reminding me that, while there is suffering everywhere, we can always do something.*

Wally survived that hospital stay and lived another couple of years. At the end of his life, he and Juanita moved into my Greenfield home for several months for access to convenient sources of heat and light, ample support on an hourly basis, and hot, running water.

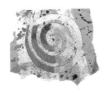

saying goodbye to Wally

Wally lived with manageable prostate cancer for about twenty years. In 2001, when he was ninety-two, the cancer became more aggressive. Doctors spoke of weeks or months.

The small group of supporters and advisors closest to the Nelsons suggested moving them to a site with modern conveniences. We strategized to anticipate and respect the Nelsons' wishes. We proposed the center of Greenfield as accessible for hospice personnel and helpful community members alike.

At the time, I shared a home with the man who would become my son's father. John owns a two-family Greenfield house located near Baystate Franklin Medical Center. He graciously agreed to make the first-floor apartment available. John's generosity allowed a support network to coalesce in order to make Wally's final chapters as comfortable as possible.

We moved the Nelsons in with the help of friends. We borrowed a hospital bed for Wally and a single bed for Nita. We brought in rockers, a shower chair, and a telephone line. At times, a party atmosphere took hold. People from many parts of the country came to pay their respects. Wally basked in the attention. Juanita, customarily ambivalent, alternately enjoyed and tolerated the stream of visitors.

Hospice professionals provided medical care and moral support. Friends contributed meals, laundry help, transportation for Juanita's outings, and companionship for Wally, thus creating a thriving version of the beloved community.

The Nelsons moved in with Eveline in March, 2002,
toward the end of Wally's life.

Nita mentioned one day that she wanted to go to their place in Deerfield to collect a few things. I had given my car away the year before, so I found a friend to take Nita up to Woolman Hill. She returned with a dark blue shoebox filled with photographs and handed the collection to me. "I've been meaning to organize these for years—never enough time. You might try pulling them out when Wally seems restless. The pictures might distract him in a nice way."

A few days later, I noticed Wally sighing during a gap between visitors. He rested in a recliner under several blankets. His skeletal frame could no longer retain warmth, and we supplemented central heating with water bottles, heating pads, and layers of quilts.

"Nita brought this box of photos down from the hill, Wally," I said, adjusting his pillows. "I recognize some of these folks but not all. Would you like to look at them with me?"

He perked up, regaling me with stories about activists he met through marches, campaigns, and boycotts. He indicated people he met through bus rides to challenge racial segregation in the late forties. He pointed to images of Maurice "Mac" McCrackin and former Ohio housemates Ernest and Marion Bromley, with whom he and Nita shared a passion for antiwar protests, including tax resistance.

I handed him photo after photo while attempting to take mental notes during a rich historical crash course.

"Whoa," I said, "this is you and . . . "

"Martin King," Wally nodded. He never spoke Dr. King's middle name but always referred to the civil rights icon as Martin King or Martin.

Some people are surprised to learn that, according to many sources, Dr. King kept guns in his Alabama home during the 1950s. Wally reminisced about the guns and more when he saw the old photo.

Wally Nelson, left, visited with Martin Luther King Jr. in the 1950s.

The photo shows the two men in front of a clapboard house. At five feet, seven inches, Dr. King stands a few inches taller than Wally and seems to slouch a bit, perhaps to deemphasize the height difference. Hands in his pockets, Wally wears a clean white T-shirt and khakis. Dr. King wears a crisp button-down short-sleeved shirt and pressed dark pants. Uncharacteristically, he looks vague.

"Martin and I had a long talk that day," Wally explained. "I asked him how a nonviolent activist could sleep with a gun under his pillow. Of course, Martin and his family were targeted by many people and groups. But I needed to challenge him on that point."

Referring to the fear civil right activists lived with day and night, Wally said, "We never knew if we'd live to see daylight.

But I decided that I would not allow fear to paralyze me. I did not tell Martin what to do. I simply asked him questions that seemed pertinent to our movement."

Apparently, Dr. King replied, "Wally, I agree with you in principle, but I'm not ready to relinquish my firearm. I know I would feel better in my soul if I did, and perhaps I will come to that point. I will consider your words carefully. Thank you for challenging me." The two went on to discuss many other aspects of the movement.

Noting Wally's relaxed stance and Dr. King's wistful expression, I studied the photo.

"Martin was an extraordinary man," Wally said, "and a powerful speaker. But there were many other organizers who risked their lives and devoted themselves to the movement. They should also be celebrated. I'm not generally a fan of special days or special months, because I believe we should actively celebrate and bring justice every single day. But I could celebrate Bayard Rustin Day. Oh, that man could sing. And he masterminded the 1963 march in Washington but was shoved to the back when it came time to give credit, because he was gay." Wally shook his head.

I picked up another photo. "Oh, my," I said, bringing the photo over to the window to study it in better light. "Is this . . . ?"

Wally reached for the photo and nodded. "I took this picture of Rosa Parks and her mother, Leona, after I met them at Highlander. They were terrific." Gesturing and emphasizing two words, he slipped his right hand out from under the blankets. "Terrific people."

Myles Horton and Don West founded Highlander Folk School in 1932 in New Market, Tennessee, to focus on organized labor, economic justice, and ending racial discrimination.

The photo shows two women in front of a brick home. Rosa Parks wears a short-sleeved floral blouse and a skirt with pockets.

Leona McCauley, left, and Rosa Parks took a moment together at the Highlander Center in Tennessee in the 1950s.

Her hands are behind her back, her hair braided or coiled atop her head. Her expression looks determinedly calm.

Her mother is slightly taller and wears a long-sleeved, lightweight dress with a Peter-Pan collar and nine buttons from throat to waist. With hands clasped in front, she seems to squint, or perhaps Wally captured her image between blinks.

"These are wonderful photos, Wally. I love the stories, too."

"Would you like to have some of the pictures?" he offered. "Show them to the kids you work with. Tell them the stories." Wally knew I worked with after-school programs. He paused. "We've been meaning to organize the pictures into albums, but there are always too many projects at home."

I felt a pang, knowing that Wally had seen his home for the last time. Never again would I help him pull the rustic tripod from beneath the house nor set up the scale to weigh produce for market. Never again would I split wood with the man who taught me how to wield an ax, nor would we fetch water together from the well.

I tried to cheer myself by anticipating days filled with stories and love in advance of Wally's inevitable departure. There was no way around it. I tried to make my peace, but I knew his exit would leave a hole in our community and in my life.

Two weeks prior to Wally's death, Amandla singers headed to my home following a performance at the local jail. We would serenade our old friend once again.

After a few songs, Wally asked, "Are we free? Am I free?" He whispered, "I don't know."

I reflected on his remarkable life. When he was a small boy, Wally ran home crying because someone called him a [n-word].

Pastor Nelson sternly asked his eleventh child, "Are you a [n-word]?"

Wally shook his head.

"What is the problem, then?" Pastor Nelson's words reverberated in Wally for the next eight decades.

Along with other Methodist youth, Wally took a pledge in his teens not to kill or use violence in any form. Wally held fast to that pledge through many wars and conflicts.

Wally refused to fight or cooperate in even the smallest way during World War II and spent three years in prison for his resistance. Despite their power and might, neither generals nor politicians could bend him to their will.

Wally's minister visited him in prison one time, saying, "Young man, you are a disgrace! What are you doing in jail?"

Wally replied, "Pastor, you told me stories about Christ. I believed your stories, but I guess you didn't. Why, you ask, am I in here? Why, I ask, are you out there?"

When skin color determined seating on public transportation according to sinister habits and laws of this nation, Wally and fifteen others acted boldly, putting themselves at great risk. Because he was truly free, Wally began dismantling the behemoth Jim Crow by testing the 1946 Irene Morgan US Supreme Court decision. He participated in the first Freedom Rides.

Wally maintained a steady course throughout the so-called patriotism and blind obedience of the 1950s and 60s. He took his convictions beyond carrying signs, marching, and signing petitions. He fasted for many days to support farm workers. He refused to budge from segregated public places. His actions led to more stints in jail and weeks of confinement in a mental hospital.

No one could dictate Wally's behavior or choices: he made his own decisions. No one forced him to act contrary to his principles: he decided what he would or would not do. At around age sixty, Wally left the city and rediscovered his rural roots. He and Juanita unplugged from the grid for nearly thirty years, living a rich and beautiful life growing their own food and washing up with homemade soap. They left a tiny footprint on the earth in an era of over-consumption and environmental devastation. They knew true freedom.

Wally's body carried him to hundreds of meetings, marches, and conferences. He weathered countless campaigns, sit-ins, and picket lines. Yet bodies wear out, and Wally's was no exception. His physical strength faded, and in his last days, he wondered whether he was truly free. Headlines screamed that the world was in a mess. Had all of Wally's work been in vain?

I leaned in to answer Wally's question. "Hundreds of people are deeply moved and motivated by your example. You inspire people simply by being yourself. You're leaving the world a better place than you found it, my friend."

Wally looked at me and then at the singers circling his bed. Sighing, he closed his eyes.

"Humanity contains a stubborn streak, a strain of courage that's bound to win out in the end," I continued. "It's because of people like you, Wally."

I pointed to proof of his status as a free man. Despite the fact that he and Nita had no biological children, he lay surrounded by people he'd befriended and mentored. Accompanied by the love of his life, he lived out his last months in a comfortable private home. Community members felt honored to hold him in our embrace and accompany him as best we could on his final journey. Not only was he free. He had burst the bonds of racism and defied the conditions of his ancestors' enslavement as devoted admirers took care of him.

"Wally, you are truly free." I said. "I will miss you terribly. But you will always be with me. You have done your job, and I must do mine."

To the sweet singers, I murmured, "Wally has planted seeds of freedom in us."

Fourteen pairs of loving hands rested lightly on Wally. We expressed our gratitude to a great soul.

Our good friend Bob Bady frequently came down from Brattleboro, Vermont, to help out. He met the Nelsons when he was eighteen, and they loved him dearly. One morning, Nita said wistfully to Bob and me, "I wish I could lay in bed with Wally one last time. One last snuggle." After they had shared a bed for more than fifty years, she couldn't bear the separation imposed by Wally's need for a hospital bed.

Bob and I looked at each other and nodded. "We can do it, Nita," I said. "We'll move Wally over and help you get in to the bed comfortably."

Her eyes became moist. "I don't know why it's so important to me. I'm an old woman having a hard time letting go. But if we can manage, I'd love it."

Bob's training as a registered nurse came in handy as we shifted Wally. We released a rail on the hospital bed to allow Nita to climb in and got her situated before returning the rail to its position. We pulled the bed sheet and dark green wool blanket to their chins. Juanita's expression softened. She closed her eyes, resting her forehead below Wally's ear. Wally opened his eyes wide and grinned as we backed out of the room, closing the French doors.

Chuck Matthei was like a son to the Nelsons. For several decades, he intertwined his life with theirs in beautiful and powerful ways. The founder of the Institute for Community Economics (ICE) and later of Equity Trust, Chuck devoted his life to pursuing economic justice and environmental stewardship.

Equity Trust aims to change the way people think about and hold property. Chuck educated people throughout the US about land trusts and other alternatives to private property ownership. Wally and Juanita took fierce pride in Chuck's accomplishments and considered him their closest advisor.

Chuck contended with cancer that year, too, and lasted only a few months after Wally's death. Chuck stayed with us for the last few weeks of Wally's life, bringing his Irish setter, Pete, to join our household, as well.

On Thursday evening, May 23, it was clear that Wally approached his end. Juanita, Chuck, and I kept vigil as Wally's breathing grew shallow. Nita alternately spoke quietly to Wally and silently held his hand.

Using a stethoscope, I heard Wally's heart slow to several beats per minute. I marveled that the human body continues to function with so little power. As Wally hovered at the precipice, Nita said, "You're a good man, Wally. You are my dear love."

When Wally left us, we remained with his body for a long time. Then Nita said she needed a hot bath. Chuck went to bed. As instructed, I called the hospice office. They told me a nurse would come by to sign the death pronouncement.

The nurse arrived around midnight. I showed her to Wally's bedside. Her manner struck me as briskly efficient after the quiet slowness of the evening. I found it jarring to integrate a person I'd never met into my new reality of life without Wally.

She pulled back the blanket to examine his body and exclaimed, "Oh, he was a little guy!"

Raw grief brought surges of protest. "Believe me," I countered, "if you knew him, you'd understand why he was the biggest man I ever met."

The nurse smiled gently. "Forgive me," she said in a quieter voice. "I did not have the pleasure of meeting him. I'm sure he was wonderful."

Her kind words unleashed in me a torrent of tears. She signed the paper, patted my arm, and let herself out as I emptied my grief into the wool blanket.

An hour later, a knock on the door announced two police officers requesting separate, brief interviews with Juanita and me. Each home death in Massachusetts requires police involvement to rule out foul play. "He was ninety-three," I told the officers, tearfully. "He had cancer for years and moved in here a couple of months ago to die in peace and comfort." Apparently, Juanita said essentially the same thing. The officers left as quickly as they'd arrived.

The next day, we filled the room with flowers and candles. "Wally lies in state," whispered a friend. Many loved ones and fans came by. Dabbing tears, they hugged Juanita.

In the spirit of do-it-ourselves, we discussed transporting Wally's body to the Eternal Flame Crematorium near Brattleboro, Vermont. A friend admonished, "You'd better get permission from town hall. You can get into a load of trouble if you don't jump through the right hoops."

Reflecting on her history of protest, Juanita said that she found the possibility of running afoul of the law in this way amusing. Still, we agreed to toe the line.

Chuck went to town hall and met resistance. He knew his rights and stated them clearly. Yet, he continued to receive pushback. Finally, Chuck announced, "Today is Friday before Memorial Day weekend. Please give me the permission I seek, or I will bring the body here and put it on your desk. You can deal with the corpse on Tuesday morning after the holiday."

As with most statements that emanated from Chuck's mouth or pen, this one came off as emphatic and authoritative. Even strangers could tell when Chuck wasn't kidding. He received permission with the stipulation that he comply with Commonwealth law and obtain a prescription from Wally's physician for a body bag.

On Saturday, we zipped the "little guy" — the greatest man I ever knew — into a grey body bag and loaded him into the back seat of Bob's truck. As we headed north, I held Wally's head in my lap. My rational mind understood that he was gone. Nonetheless, I gave in to the urge to unzip the bag so that the morning sun might play across his magnificent face one last time.

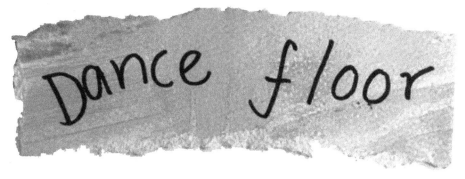

During one of Wally's hospital stays, I witnessed a beautiful scene. Juanita did a simple thing every bit as powerful as a protest or boycott. She rejoiced.

Nita took Wally's hand after sliding a cassette tape into the player. Music filled the room, and she began to dance with Wally.

Famous for cutting the rug, even at ninety, Wally left women a quarter his age gasping for breath. But now it was all Wally could do to open his eyes.

Although Wally lay immobilized, Nita danced with him as though they were at a swanky dance club. Feet gliding over the floor, Nita's shoulders alternated sensuously to the beat. Wally opened his eyes. He whispered, "Jitterbug." Nita threw her head back in laughter and kept dancing.

Witnessing the Nelsons' courage in saying "No" to injustice and destruction inspired me. Yet, equally inspiring was another kind of courage that says "Yes" to celebration even in tough moments.

The courage Juanita displayed that evening streamed from a solid source that provides the guts to live life to the fullest.

Soon after Wally died, we did a show with Juanita. Stepping to the podium, Juanita gestured to the singers standing behind her. "You provide the soundtrack for my stories," she said. "Thank you for singing for Wally so many times before he left us!"

Just Juanita

Juanita continued to collaborate with Amandla after Wally's death in 2002. I introduced her at a show for high school students.

Juanita Nelson is well-known for the kind of courage that will not bow in the face of injustice. Juanita refused to budge from segregated restaurants and stood up in the face of Klan violence in Georgia. She consistently says no to oppression based on skin color. In 1940, at age sixteen, Juanita defied a law dictating segregation on interstate trains.

Juanita's first instance of breaking the law was not part of an organized action. During a trip south with her mother to visit family, Juanita grew dismayed upon passing into a state where it was illegal for people of different skin shades to sit in the same train car.

Yearning for common sense and justice, the defiant teen spontaneously decided to travel the length of the train to sit briefly in each car. She received frightened looks from brown-skinned folks and angry ones from whites, but no one challenged her directly. Perhaps no one wanted to confront a young person so clearly in charge of herself.

Juanita Nelson commits many acts of defiance. At eighty, she continues to live in ways that inspire others. She insists, "I just do what makes sense to me."

Please help me welcome Juanita Nelson.

The applause was deafening.

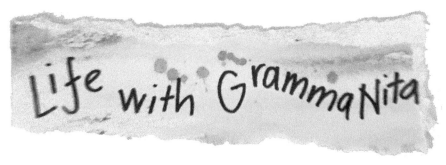

Life with Gramma Nita

Two years after Wally died, the arrival of Gillis deepened my relationship with Juanita. She accompanied me through parts of my long labor, and when the baby finally arrived, Nita saw his face before I did.

A long history of lost pregnancies contributed to my sense of celebration. I couldn't believe my wild luck as I labored with Nita at my side and enjoyed being serenaded by a quartet of Amandla singers. Rebecca, Laura, Barbara, and Steve brought musical magic when I needed it most. I highly recommend a soundtrack of gentle, live music for women settling in for a day and a half of labor.

Steve Cobb, Laura Stell, Rebecca Speisman, and Barbara Buschner, from left,
help sing Eveline through labor in May, 2004.
Micah Snow-Cobb, right, brought moral support.

Nita was part of Gillis's family from the start. When he
formed words, he dubbed her GrammaNita. Their bond grew
both at the Bean Patch, the Woolman Hill farm Nita called home,
and at our Greenfield home, where Nita lived for several stints.

During his toddler years, Gillis loved riding in our bike cart
for weekly visits to Woolman Hill. I don't know who invented
contraptions to transport children behind bicycles, but the feature
allowing parents to snap heavy, transparent plastic down while
pulling kids behind them in order to protect the little ones from
wind and rain is sheer genius. It enabled me to visit Nita with
a small child in tow no matter what the weather. Tucked in
with blankets and sometimes a hot water bottle, my kiddo rode
contentedly while I did the pedaling.

Gillis loved doing chores for Gram. The well enthralled him, and he often observed that, "Gwam needs wah-doo." His favorite moment came when the bailer hit the water's surface, delivering the familiar "glug glug glug, SUCK," cuing us to pull up and empty the bailer into the bucket.

When Gillis outgrew the bike cart and graduated to our tandem, he gloried in the four-mile jaunt up the hill. Pre-motherhood, throughout my twenties and thirties, I proudly resisted the temptation to hop off the bike and walk the last, steepest incline on the way to the Bean Patch. Left to my own devices in my advancing forties, I happily would have wimped out, but Gillis took up the can-do spirit from his seat behind mine, yelling, "Come on, Mama! Don't quit! We can do it!" The rousing cheering section made it impossible to give in to my weaker self.

During our visits, Gillis divided his time between hanging out with the older folks and ranging off on his own to explore the woods and fields surrounding Nita's cabin. I felt confident that he was safe when we were up at Nita's. The hole for the well was far too small for him to fall into, and there were no other clear or present dangers I could think of.

One time, however, when Gillis was four, and we needed to head back to town, and I couldn't find him anywhere. I checked the woodshed, the back room, the tomato patch, and the corn crib that served as a tool shed. Finally, I yelled, "Gillis, if you can hear me, I need you to answer me right now! This is really important!"

A small voice responded, "I'm up here, Mama." Having discovered the wooden ladder to Nita's roof, he'd climbed up and just sat there in his little yellow windbreaker, taking it all in. It became a favorite pursuit during visits. He looked like a miniature meditator sitting up there.

Gillis loved to fill GrammaNita's wood box. I passed on to him a skill I learned from Wally and taught my son to split wood

Gillis removed his bike helmet at a stop but always wore it on the road!
He loved riding up Woolman Hill in the bike cart to visit GrammaNita.
His Mama loved when he got old enough to help pedal up the steep hill.

at the age of five. It made a great impression on him and set the tone for his sixth birthday party.

Each year, we chose a theme in honor of his birthday. When he turned five, he requested that his friends have the opportunity to play the clarinet, the bassoon, and the trumpet at his party. Other years, themes included baseball, trampoline jumping, trains, and playing in the sprinkler.

In advance of his sixth birthday, I asked, "What special thing would you like for your party this year?"

He responded with gravity. "I think it's important for kids to know how to split wood. Can we have a wood-splitting party?"

I recoiled, imagining severed digits and massive blood loss. My mother's father lost three toes in an accident involving a pile of wood and an ax. "Can we think of something a little more . . . safe, Honey?"

"Splitting wood is perfectly safe when you take your time and stay focused," he said, repeating what he'd heard from me many times.

It's hard to argue with common sense. Several children learned to split wood on a Saturday afternoon in May before the annual DIY decorating of homemade cake with flowers from our garden. I went to bed that night giving thanks for the bevy of adults who helped keep the kids safe and focused.

During the times GrammaNita lived downstairs in our home, Gillis disappeared for parts of each day, and I'd find him with Gram having a snack or immersed in discussion. He also loved to bring his friends downstairs to visit with Gram. I folded laundry or worked on choral arrangements on the second floor while hearing bursts of laughter from Nita. Little kids are hilarious.

One day, members of our small home-school collective bounced on the trampoline in our yard. Four-year-old Audrey burst into the first-floor apartment where Juanita and I sat drawing up a grocery list.

Panting, Audrey exclaimed, "GrammaNita, come jump on the trampoline with us!"

"Audrey," said Nita with severe dignity, "I am eighty-seven years of age."

Audrey threw her arms around Nita's knees and exclaimed, "That's a good time to jump on the trampoline."

Nita's stern expression dissolved in waves of helpless laughter. Audrey did not succeed in coaxing Nita onto the trampoline, but she did manage to lead our dear elder outside to enjoy the sunshine and laughter of young children.

In January of 2011, I organized We're All in the Same Boat, a benefit concert to raise funds for Juanita. Community members filled the Brick Church in Old Deerfield to show their support. They contributed money and enjoyed performances from Amandla and the Green River String Band. Contending with significant memory issues, Juanita struggled somewhat to remain on track during what would be one of her last public addresses. Carl Doerner filmed the event and produced a video showing Juanita with humor and dignity intact.

After the concert, Juanita took me aside. "You're my social security," she said. "All of you. Thank you."

The cultures I grew up in honor the deceased in ways that feel very different to me. My Québécois family attends solemn

Roman Catholic funeral masses followed by receptions filled with laughter, stories, food, and song. Memorial services I attend in the US are more eclectic—a mix of awkward, comforting, and intellectual. In either case, I find the singing always the best part.

In late January of 2014, I spent three or four days feeling weepy and lost in thought. Pete Seeger's death on January 27, just weeks after the departure of Nelson Mandela on December 5, filled me with enormous gratitude tinged with anxiety. *The mentors are dying! Who will fill the void?*

I could imagine each of those magnificent men admonishing us to keep going; movements for social change do not hinge on any one person. Still, it can be painfully deflating to bid farewell to those who have lit the way with astonishing courage and prodigious energy. Singing helps me at such times.

Our chorus occasionally devotes a rehearsal session to honoring the passing of a great soul. We invite community members to join us in song and remembrance. We do not think of them as memorial services per se. Rather, they are song fests to raise the roof, make room for tears, and bring us together.

Following Mandela's death, I learned of a large gathering planned in his honor at UMass Amherst within a couple of months and felt honored by the invitation for Amandla to participate. When I learned of Pete's death, I knew many events would spring up, given the large number of people in the Pioneer Valley who counted Pete as a friend. The tribute hosted by Amandla was one of many in our area.

For me, the toughest farewell took place after Juanita Nelson died on March 9, 2015. Mandela had inspired me for many years, and I loved meeting him on one occasion. Pete became a friend as well as a colleague. But Juanita was my intimate friend, a housemate on several occasions, and (along with Wally) truly an additional parent.

The official celebration of Juanita's life was scheduled for the end of May. I knew it would be wonderful and was grateful to all involved with the planning. Yet I needed a Juanita Song Fest as soon as possible following her death, and many people shared that wish.

More than a hundred people gathered in our rehearsal space on March 24, and we sang to celebrate the remarkable lives of both Juanita and Wally. Many in attendance had worked with the Nelsons on projects related to agriculture, land trusts, tax resistance, and more.

"Swing down, chariot, stop an' let me ride!" The song I learned from Ysaye Barnwell boomed through the space. We continued at the top of our lungs: "Gonna lay down my sword and shield, down by the riverside," a song we shared with the Nelsons at many protests and rallies.

"We're Marchin' on to Freedom Land" and "Guide My Feet" brought to mind photos and stories of Wally and Juanita on picket lines, emerging from jail, and holding signs.

We sang "This Little Light of Mine," "Amazing Grace," "We Shall Not Be Moved," and Wally's all-time favorite, "Oh, Freedom."

"Freedom Agitation," words from Frederick Douglass that I set to music, seemed a fitting way to remember Juanita and Wally: "Those who profess to favor freedom but deprecate agitation are those who want crops without plowing the ground."

With tears and smiles, we sang without speeches or eulogies.

We wrapped up with three beautiful songs: Peggy Seeger's "Love Call Me Home" (arranged by the musical powerhouse Peter Amidon); David Dodson's "Farthest Field" (arranged by another southern Vermont talent, Mary Cay Brass); and "Precious Lord" by Thomas A. Dorsey, a great favorite of Juanita's.

Many times as Wally was dying, and later, as she, too, neared life's end, Juanita observed in an amused tone: "I'm not sure where I get all this religion, seeing as I'm an atheist, but these old hymns really do it for me!"

ChoQosh Auh'ho'oh and the Elders

After September 11, 2001 — and long before I participated in the internet — a friend handed me a print-out of something he'd found online. "Some Hopi elders just issued this statement," he said. "You might like it. Maybe you'll set it to music?"

I did set it to music, naming the composition "The Elders." Amandla performed it locally to great reviews, but I was reluctant to record it, since I wasn't positive about the source. An internet-savvy friend, Will, warned me about the high volume of bogus material online, and helped me do some digging. Our research led me to ChoQosh Auh'ho'oh, a California coastal Chumash elder.

I spoke with ChoQosh by phone a few years after I set the elders' words to music. Our initial two-hour conversation on April 9, 2006, impacted me enormously. ChoQosh immediately debunked the myth that the Hopi elders had issued the statement after 9/11. She explained the actual sources and gave me permission to share her story.

I took copious notes during our lengthy phone conversations. ChoQosh's stories are filled with wisdom, confusion, warnings, and hope. In her words, this is what she told me:

When I was in my early twenties and had two small children, I lived with the Hopi in Oraibi, Arizona. Elders taught me the Hopi Prophecy in 1966 and 1967.

Later, during the seventies and eighties, I taught workshops called Eleventh-Hour Tools for Spiritual Warriors. Some people didn't like my use of the word warrior, but I did some research and found that a soldier is someone who acts on the truth of others, while a warrior lives from personal truth and whose life is a search for truth.

I refer to the Eleventh Hour as a time of purification. I was very active throughout the eighties, including taking on the Vatican in 1985 to protest the canonization of a priest who was associated with killing and subjugating many indigenous people and who set up concentration camps in the hopes of erasing their cultures.

Around this time, many Native American elders were slandered and attacked. The source of these attacks seemed to come from an elusive organization which claimed to safeguard Native spirituality by denouncing various people. Yet, the organization was impossible to pinpoint or confront. Whoever they were, they had a lot of money and produced very slick material. This made me suspicious, because most indigenous groups don't have two nickels to rub together.

In 1988, I was driving with a dear friend when we were rear-ended by a car that drove away at a high speed. My friend died in that hit-and-run incident, and I was critically injured. In fact, the EMTs initially pronounced me dead at the scene but detected vital signs en route to the hospital. I was in the ICU for many months and not expected to live. While in the hospital, though, I had a vision of a tree growing up out of my belly. After that vision, I made a remarkable recovery, astonishing the doctors.

I went back to doing my radio show, *Songs for the Earth*, and one day brought in the famous medicine man, Rolling Thunder. After the broadcast, I described to Rolling Thunder my experience in the ICU. He chuckled and slapped my thigh, yelling, "Girl, that was the Tree of Life!"

In 1993, I was fifty-one and living in Willets, California, about three hours north of San Francisco. I decided to go back to college in Mendocino to major in Psychology of Community Building: Its Art and Implementation.

While in school, I learned that there was a slick packet of slander making the rounds, accusing me of selling Hopi secrets. I began to wonder if I had, indeed, been an affront to the Hopi elders with whom I'd lived and learned? I had been told that the wisdom was given to me in order to share, but perhaps I had acted inappropriately?

As I dealt with intense confusion, something surfaced in my house that I hadn't seen for many years: my address book from the 1960s. I opened the book to a page showing the phone number for Thomas Banyacya.

Banyacya (1909–1999), a Hopi elder and Native American traditional leader, was one of four Hopis named by elders to reveal Hopi traditional wisdom and teachings — including prophecies for the future — to the general public after the atomic bombings of the Japanese cities of Hiroshima and Nagasaki. Elders also chose David Monongye, Dan Evehema, and Dan Katchongva for the task. Banyacya belonged to the Wolf, Fox, and Coyote clans.

Thomas Banyacya's number was written in pencil, barely legible by that time, and I had to guess at a couple of digits. Yet when I dialed the number, Thomas answered on the first ring and spoke as if we were in the middle of a conversation. He said, "Come right way! The elders want to speak with you!"

Overwhelmed by schoolwork, with papers to write and research to do, I felt torn and panicked. But since it was a Friday preceding a week off from classes, I got in my car and began my thousand-mile journey to the Third Mesa.

I arrived in Oraibi and stayed at the home of Thomas and his wife, Fermina. I spent the week being treated as if I was unwelcome. I slept in a tiny storage room. I was told nothing. My hosts barely spoke to me. I wondered if I'd lost my mind on a wild goose chase. I fretted about the schoolwork awaiting me.

After nearly a week, I figured I'd head back to California. But Fermina came to me and said, "There's someone here to see you." I went outside and saw Dolly Jackson, daughter of John Lansa.

John Lansa had been the chief in the time I lived there. Dolly directed me to go to the chief's house. Then she left. But no one answered the door, so I ended up sleeping in my station wagon, right in front of the chief's house.

I awakened just before dawn in Oraibi, one of the oldest continuously inhabited settlements in the western hemisphere. The people there are very poor, just as they were in the time I'd lived there. I looked around at the poverty and the beauty of the place, watching in awe as the most beautiful sunrise I've ever seen unfolded before my eyes. Deep oranges and reds were split in half by the deepest purple. I knew my car was parked right over a kiva, an underground room used for spiritual ceremonies.

I felt all the confusion of my journey, yet I also felt the wonder and sacredness of this place. Still, I had no answers about why I'd been summoned. I figured I'd watch the remainder of the sunrise and then get back in my car and head home. I realized in that moment that this could signal the end of a chapter in my life that was marked by my association with the Hopi. I wondered what was next for me and what it all meant?

I glanced around and did something I'd never before done on a reservation: I reached for my camera. One is not supposed to take pictures on the rez. I told myself it was all right since I was going to photograph the sunrise and not the rez itself.

I heard a movement from behind me and tossed my camera into the car, hoping I hadn't been seen. I turned around.

Interestingly, I never found that camera again.

Several elders approached, led by two men, one of whom was obviously the oldest. The other lead fellow looked to be in his fifties. No one acknowledged my presence. Then, without looking at me, the older one said, "You have been telling people this is the Eleventh Hour."

I had learned the phrase on that very reservation. I opened my mouth to ask if I shouldn't have shared the teaching, but the elder continued to speak without looking at me. "Now we tell you it is the hour, and there are things to be considered. Where do you live? What is it that you are doing?"

He continued, "What are your relationships? What is it you are in relationship to? Are you in right relation?"

He paused, then went on. "Where is your water? Know your garden. It is time to speak your truth. Create your community. Be good to each other. And do not look outside yourself for the leader."

He clapped and squeezed his hands. "This could be a good time!"

The elders began a procession. They still hadn't fully acknowledged me, so I called out desperately, "There's a lot of trouble going on! Were the things I learned here just for me? Or to share?"

The elders slowed their procession but didn't stop. Without looking at me, the eldest said, "Do you remember when you were here before? You were told three things to remember. Do you remember?"

I nodded quickly, wanting to be in his good graces, but then I panicked. I had learned so many teachings — and many of them in threes. I wondered desperately which three he meant? I kicked myself for letting my ego take the lead. I knew I should just admit I wasn't sure exactly which three he meant.

Suddenly, my mind became clear. I said, "Wake up and be aware. Ask permission. Then it's up to you."

I had my answer. I'd already fulfilled those three, and the elders were telling me I hadn't done anything wrong. They continued their procession and then just walked away.

Dolly Jackson came back for me and took me to a sacred kachina dance and ceremony. Then I got back in my car and drove through the night, back home to California.

I asked ChoQosh where the rest of the text came from? She explained:

The other parts didn't come from that day. The rest may come from Uncle John, an Iroquois elder, and/or Grandfather Victor, or possibly from Grandmother Twylah Nitsch, from the Seneca clan. I think the part about "We are the ones we have been waiting for . . . " comes from a poem. I'm not sure.

A few weeks after I spoke with ChoQosh, I discovered that "We are the ones we have been waiting for . . . " comes from a June Jordan poem. I asked whether she thought it was all right to put words from varying sources together.

Her response was, "All of that wisdom is meant to be chanted or sung." And then, sharing a piece of Maori wisdom, ChoQosh added, "Music gives words wings."

Toward the end of one of our phone calls, ChoQosh said,
I have told it to you. Now you are in the lineage, my love. You are in the lineage of the Tellers of the Story. I have given you the complete story, and you have my permission to pass it on.

Ten years after hatching Amandla, I dreamed of starting another community project. At the time, the two endeavors seemed unrelated, but I came to see that grassroots entities tend to complement each other. A newspaper item about a community garden across the river in nearby Turners Falls inspired me to launch a similar project in Greenfield. I consulted with Suzette Snow-Cobb, a dear friend who helped start the Great Falls Community Garden on Fourth Street.

During my first decade in Greenfield, I lived in a series of small apartments. I squeezed plants into tiny outdoor spaces while longing for a real garden plot. I felt kinship when I first heard the term landless peasant.

Family history shows that my gardening urge comes from both sides. For nine generations, my mother's people have farmed in St. Germain de Grantham, Québec, a tradition that continues as my cousin Denis Janelle with his wife, Sylvie Soucy

Community gardeners stop for a picnic break during a work day.
Founding members Gregg Crawford and Dorothea Sotiros, front,
contributed many hours.

and their sons own and operate Le Pépinière Janelle. Pépinière means nursery, and my cousins run their business with ingenuity and perseverance. I urge readers who find themselves on Route 122 to stop in at Le Pépinière and say "Bonjour."

My father raised a wide variety of vegetables in our yard. Each year, we aimed to harvest a first red tomato during that brief period when just enough unbolted lettuce remains to make a "green and red" on toasted bread with gobs of mayonnaise. Each summer, Dad lived in his garden with a trowel, watering can, and transistor radio so he could listen to baseball games.

The history of the Pleasant Street Community Garden is complex. I laud the enormous amount of energy and heart many people brought to the project. Coordinating the community garden

Eveline, neighborhood kids, and community gardeners take a workday break.

for more than a decade—a volunteer post—provided me with valuable lessons in organizing, cross-cultural awareness, party planning, organic practices, and many other aspects related to horticulture, human nature, crisis management, and celebration.

I walked or biked to the garden early each morning, grateful for permission from the town of Greenfield and the school committee to utilize land on the grounds of the Davis Street School. The beautiful old brick building housed school administrative offices until the town razed the building in 2017 to make way for the new senior center.

Each morning, I scanned the site for dog poop, trash, and evidence of vandalism. One Saturday, I surveyed the scene with satisfaction. Aside from a few food wrappers, the coast was clear. I felt mystified, however, by scraping sounds coming from nearby. Crossing the deserted street to the driveway of an apartment building, I discovered a thirty-something woman on her hands and knees in a tiny triangular patch of dirt. Using a metal dustpan, she scraped soil aside, shook seeds from a packet, covered them, and poured water from a beige plastic pitcher onto the bedraggled site. She didn't notice me at first. I stood nearby, witnessing confirmation of the fact that when dedicated gardeners wish to work the soil, they will do so wherever possible.

Quietly, I cleared my throat. She looked up, embarrassed. I introduced myself and learned her chosen Anglo name, Lisa. A recent immigrant from China, she spoke little English and dashed into the building to fetch her husband, a Chinese fellow wearing glasses. He introduced himself as Bill. A chemical engineer, he had dual language skills that allowed Lisa and me to converse. Describing my role as coordinator of the community garden, I offered her a plot located just a few steps from her home.

Lisa covered a grin with her hands. "She has been wanting to know about that garden," her husband said, "but didn't know who to ask."

I invited them to accompany me across the street, where I showed them a ten-foot-by-twenty-foot plot, saying, "If you'd like it, this is yours."

Blinking back tears, Lisa shook her head affirmatively and spoke in rapid-fire phrases to her husband. Bill translated.

Starting young: little Zephyr greets the newest community garden member, Eveline's son Gillis, in 2004.

Suzy Polucci, a founding member, visits Juanita Nelson's farmer's market booth to purchase pansies for the community garden.

"She cannot believe it. She can grow so much food here." As his wife shivered with excitement, Bill added, "This makes her very happy." He beamed at Lisa, who still held the metal dustpan in one hand.

Pointing to the tool shed, I urged, "Come see where we keep shovels, rakes, and other equipment." I demonstrated how to open the combination lock. "Please feel free to use any of these tools. Just put them back when you're done and lock the door."

Lisa stared at the rows of implements and giggled, hiding the dustpan behind her back.

"I mean, it's a nice dust pan," I said, "but, you know, maybe not the best thing for gardening." Bill laughed, and Lisa nodded, smiling, after he translated.

I shook hands with each of them and explained that I planned to drop off an orientation packet later in the day. "Everything you need to know about being a member is in the packet," I said. "Phone numbers, agreements, information about work days, gardening tips. I look forward to introducing you to other members. Welcome to the community garden."

They thanked me and, chatting excitedly, made their way back across the street toward their home.

Young farmers Micah Snow-Cobb and Gillis MacDougall prepare to help move a shipment of mulching straw in 2007.

Within a few months, Lisa conversed in basic English with ease. Recalling my mother's process of learning the challenging language, I cheered Lisa on as we shared gardening concerns and victories.

I grew fond of all the gardeners, but as the daughter of an immigrant, I reserved a special place in my heart for those who courageously adopted the US as their new home. I learned Hindi words for various vegetables from a wonderful extended family and marveled at farming skills they brought from their village in northern India.

Maria, from Moldova, demonstrated how to construct fantastic garlic wreaths. While I fumbled, she worked swiftly with deft flicks of her wrists. She taught me the word for garlic, which sounded like "oosteroy."

Recently transplanted from Ukraine, eighty-three-year-old Zina kindly tolerated my elementary attempts at Russian greetings as I searched my memory banks for phrases from two long-ago semesters of study.

Zina soon supplemented my meager Russian vocabulary with a few Ukrainian words, but more than anything, she wanted to practice English. One warm afternoon, Zina beckoned from where she sat on an overturned five-gallon plastic bucket, weeding the plot where four generations of her family grew produce.

Reaching deep into a pocket of her smock-like dress, Zina glanced around the garden as if to make certain no one was watching. From her pocket, she pulled a red silk handkerchief folded into a little bundle. She drew closer to me.

Gillis and his friend Wylie jam at one of many community garden workdays that invariably turned into parties.

"Sids," she whispered. "From homm."

Initially, I didn't get it. With a delicate touch, Zina arranged the corners of the bundle to reveal a small pile of seeds.

"Oh, Zina," I exhaled. "Seeds from Ukraine. You saved them and brought them here."

Reaching for my hand, she deposited a pinch of seeds in my left palm. "For you. Love. Garden." She rolled her Rs beautifully.

My eyes welled up so that the seeds swam before me as I tried to thank her. "Zina, dyakuyu, thank you. What a wonderful gift. What kind of seeds?"

Not comprehending, Zina narrowed her eyes, shaking her head.

"Will they grow into . . . " I pointed to a small cabbage head.

Smiling, she said, "Nemaye, no, no."

I pointed to a number of different vegetables, striking out each time.

Proudly, Zina pulled herself up to her full four-foot-ten. "Own-yon," she sang out. "Own-yon sids."

"Onions. Oh, lovely," I said, holding the gift with reverence.

"Friend," Zina murmured, cocking her head to one side.

"Yes, Zina," I confirmed, gesturing to the two of us. "We are friends." After a pause, I made a request. "Will you teach me a song?"

Through songs, conversations, seeds, stories, and friendships, I travel. Some of my loved ones travel the world, and I bid them farewell with best wishes. Global peace workers like Paula Green of Karuna Center for Peacemaking earn my admiration and awe by bringing skilled compassion to global locations torn by conflict and strife.

Yet I remain rooted in community, exploring both the foreign and the familiar in the region where I've lived since 1986. New England feels like home, as does Québec, as do the Adirondacks. Mostly, I feel at home when working on community projects with other people, whether or not we share a language.

When two or more of my loves come together, that is pure heaven: music and planting, art and languages, stories and activism, homeschooling and mulching. The richness of life overwhelms me with beauty each and every day.

Wind on the bridge
An ancient love song and a new friendship

I drove to Springfield to meet with a Vietnamese woman I'd never met, a friend of a friend. Hongkiem generously agreed to host me in her home and help me with context and pronunciation for "Qua câo gió bay," an ancient folk song.

I heard James Durst sing the song when he performed at Greenfield's Green River Café where I coordinated concerts in the early 1990s. James, a collector of international folk songs and talented songwriter, traveled to Vietnam in 1974. There, James met Pham Duy (pronounced Fahm Zwee), whom he called Vietnam's Pete Seeger, and learned the hauntingly beautiful song.

"Qua câo gió bay" apparently originated around the
thirteenth century. The words mean:
> Loving you, I will give my hat to you and go home.
> I'll tell a lie to my pa and ma, saying,
> "I went across the bridge. Wind, wind, wind blew my hat
> away."
> Loving you, I will give my cloak to you and go home.
> I'll tell a lie to my pa and ma, saying,
> "I went across the bridge. Wind, wind, wind blew my cloak
> away."
> Loving you, I will give my ring to you and go home.
> I will say to my pa and ma:
> "I went across the bridge.
> "Love, love, love stole my heart away."

When I heard James sing it, I thought, *We must do this in
Amandla.* James offered tips on learning the song but encouraged
me to track down a native speaker for help.

Perennially up to my ears in sheet music, songbooks, and
recordings, I set "Qua câo gió bay" aside for a few years.

In 1998, while in Spanish language classes at Greenfield
Community College, I met a young woman named Xinh Dinh.
Xinh was born in Vietnam and emigrated to the US as a teen.
After mastering English, she took on Spanish "to get a good job."
She was happy to help me with Vietnamese pronunciation.

When I finally tried my hand at a choral arrangement in
2000, I'd lost touch with Xinh Dinh. I wanted at least one more
coaching session before attempting to teach it to Amandla singers.
I made a connection through Meme, one of the singers.

I arrived at a modest ranch house in a treeless Springfield
neighborhood. I gathered tape recorder, notebook, and a bouquet
of flowers from the passenger seat.

The door opened to reveal a slight, smiling woman. She
seemed shy, but her face lit up. "I love flowers!" she exclaimed.

I learned a great deal from my new friend over the course of several hours. She coached me in pronunciation and shared her deep love for Vietnam's people and culture. Less enthusiastically, she told me of her experiences during the war waged on her land by the US.

I asked if she might tell me a bit about resettlement camps where she'd spent time in Cambodia, adding that we could skip the topic if she preferred. Staring at her hands, she explained in a quiet voice that at times she and others resorted to eating grass. "When there was no food," she said, "we ate dirt. We boiled roots."

Her accounts of starvation stood in contrast with the sumptuous meal she served that day, bringing out each dish on a different set of plates until the dining room table looked like a feast for a dozen hungry people.

I wish I'd written down the names and ingredients of all the dishes she brought forth from the kitchen in a parade of culinary ecstasy! I remember little rolls filled with pork and shrimp, dipping sauces, salad with mint, basil, and mango. I sampled sizzling crêpe-like treats and some type of meatball, different from any meatball I'd ever eaten.

She treated me like a queen. I felt sheepish, knowing she already offered a huge favor that day by giving me her time and cultural expertise. But her smiles grew wider as each new delicacy caused me to exclaim with delight.

Clearly, the act of cooking and sharing food brought her great pleasure. But she ate not one bite. I felt awkward. I didn't want to risk offending her by being clueless about tradition or custom, but I wanted to invite her to join me in the feast. Instead, I watched as she sprang up and said, "Oh, you must try this!"

She came back with what looked like an enormous, thick-skinned grapefruit and said a word that sounded like "Byoo yoi!" She cleaved it right there at the table and sprinkled it liberally with salt. She said, "You have never eaten this, my new friend! It is so good!"

I tried not to wrinkle my nose. I'd never put salt on grapefruit, and it didn't appeal to me. After one bite, though, I was sold and crowed, "What is this? It's delicious!" (I had never heard of pomelos.)

We chatted, worked on pronunciation, and shared life stories, tears, and funny vignettes from our childhoods.

"I'm so grateful for your time," I said, "And you're such a fabulous cook!" Trying to be tactful, I added, "The food is so delicious!" And then, because she hadn't taken a bite, I said, "Won't you join me?"

Her face clouded over, and I realized I'd misstepped. Stammering, I said, "I'm enjoying it so much! Oh, I'm sorry. I've said the wrong thing."

She shook her head. "Do not be sorry, my new friend. It is not your fault." Pausing, she seemed to weigh self-consciousness with a desire to reassure. "I have many problems with my stomach. Perhaps because of my time in the camps? I have cancer. More than half of my stomach is removed."

We sat in silence. I thought, *How cruel. This lovely woman survives starvation and harrowing escapes only to find herself unable to feast when she finally reaches safety.*

"I'm so sorry," I whispered. She nodded. I added, "I wish I could do something."

"You are doing something," she said, standing to remove dishes. "You bring my childhood back to me with song. You help me to remember happier times."

Hongkiem wouldn't allow me to clear a single dish or spoon. Her teenaged son returned home, and she proudly introduced the handsome young man. She said, "This nice lady wants to learn about Vietnamese music and culture." He said hello and headed to his room.

Driving home, I vibrated with tonal sounds, harmonies, images of grandeur and desperation, and the richness of a new friendship. I completed a choral arrangement of "Qua câo gió bay" late that night and began teaching parts to Amandla singers the following week. As ever, they eagerly worked on new material, fully understanding the significance of North Americans honoring Vietnamese culture. Yet they struggled with pronunciation and some of the intervals.

I called Hongkiem several times during those rehearsal months and she was thrilled when I reported our progress. "I'm pretty sure we'll have it ready for our spring concert! You and your son will be our honored guests. You can sit right up front and keep an ear on our pronunciation!" I looked forward to recognizing her publicly.

There was silence on the line. I hastily added, "If you'd like to come, of course? There's no pressure, Hongkiem. But if transportation is an issue, we can take care of that . . . "

"In the spring," she said quietly. "That will be wonderful."

"Oh, good," I said, relieved.

I worked on the concert poster design. The phone rang. Meme, Hongkiem's dear friend, said, "I'm sorry to tell you this. Hongkiem died yesterday."

I shouldn't have felt shocked. I knew of Hongkiem's illness. But my young, wishful mind played tricks. When confronted with the possibility of losing my new friend, I fooled myself into thinking, *Of course she won't die! She's so vibrant!*

I proposed to Meme that we invite Hongkiem's son to our concert in order to pay tribute to his mother, but Meme helped me understand that it would be too public for the young, grieving fellow. She suggested, "Let's invite him to one of our final rehearsals before the big show and sing it just for him."

When Hongkiem's son arrived at our rehearsal space, Meme greeted him warmly and drew him into our circle. "Let's sing the song," she said, nodding.

The singers recognized the importance of singing the ancient love song more beautifully than ever before. All hesitation was gone and the words and harmonies flowed smoothly. The young man stared at our knees the whole time.

When the song ended, the silence felt sacred. I let it be. Then I told him, "Your mother gave us so much, so very much. We offer you all our love. Thank you for coming to be with us."

Each time we perform "Qua cầo gió bay," I see a tiny, smiling woman cleaving large, round fruit in half. She beckons me to taste something unfamiliar. She urges me to savor life and to treasure friendships and loved ones.

A few years later, I received a letter from Amandla singer Elizabeth Farnsworth telling me about her 2004 trip to Vietnam, which she undertook with family members to visit the country of her adopted niece's birth.

> What an experience for those of us who came of age in the war era of body counts, My Lai, and the evacuation from Saigon, to visit that country and to reach across what might have been irreparable wounds of history to make many friends.
>
> One way to cross that divide, of course, was music. I mentioned to our guide, Quynh (pronounced "Quinn"), that I learned an old Vietnamese love song while singing with a chorus in Massachusetts. A smile spread across his face as I sang "Qua cầo gió bay."

"That song was composed in my home province," he exclaimed. "I love that song and grew up singing it!" We sang it together, and everyone gathered around to listen. At the end, he said it was incredible to meet someone from so far away who knew that song.

New Year's Eve found us in Hoi An with the inevitable celebratory mix of tourists and locals toasting in 2005. A karaoke contest ensued with no lyrics provided but with a live band backing up anyone brave enough to perform. My family drafted me as their diva, and I began with John Lennon's "Imagine." Quynh leapt to the stage and urged me to sing "Qua câo gió bay."

The band looked pretty surprised but accompanied us ably. When we finished our duet, the master of ceremonies noted that he had never in his wildest dreams imagined that an American woman would sing a Vietnamese love song. Perhaps in that small corner of the country, I was able to build a bridge, so to speak. By learning songs from many places, we Amandla singers have opportunities to become musical ambassadors.

Women's struggles

Like most people born female in the mid twentieth century, I could write an entire book about how patriarchy, sexism, gender oppression, and societal pressures have affected me. I could write chapters like The Math Teacher Who Ignored Girls, Catholic Oppression of Females, Date Rape, No Sports for Girls, The Man Who Killed My Distant Cousin, and more.

It's heartening to witness increasing numbers of women speaking up about abuse in the work place, domestic violence, parity in athletics, and many other vital topics. Over the years, my awareness of such progress grew, in part, through my association with the New England Learning Center for Women in Transition (NELCWIT).

For many years, NELCWIT invited Amandla to sing at "Take Back the Night" rallies in Greenfield, gatherings where women (and a handful of men) chanted and waved banners upholding women's rights to respect and safety. I always wished more men would attend so the rallies would look more like the world we live in, but it felt good to get out there and sing for the rights of women to live in peace and safety.

Amandla also teamed up with NELCWIT to provide music at somber gatherings following incidents of domestic violence that took the lives of Pioneer Valley women. I grew up with the awareness that bad things happen to women, but when I learned statistics from NELCWIT and other sources, I recognized our culture is rife with such violence. The epidemic receives far less policy and media attention than it deserves, and societal structures allow the violence to continue.

I began to notice more and more the dozens of situations where misogyny plays out, including advertising, employment practices, politics, athletics, entertainment, and literature. I could scarcely bear the feelings of vulnerability it brought up for me as a young woman, but whenever NELCWIT called, Amandla answered every time. The organization's staff works in the trenches every day. I knew we had to show up and raise our voices.

It bolstered our spirits to bring rousing, upbeat songs of defiance and protest to the events, but for me, the most meaningful moments occurred when we took the energy down a few notches and sang of lament and sorrow. I poured my soul into those songs. I wanted to give voice to unanswered questions that swirled with greater intensity each time Amandla stood with loved ones mourning losses of sisters, daughters, mothers, and friends felled by violent anger and disregard.

Questions woke me at night:

Why are women and girls considered less valuable than men and boys?

Can we hope to rectify inequality when those who are oppressed are trained, from birth, to submit?

How can we address our cultural problem when successive generations of parents raise children within societal institutions pervaded by sexism and disrespect?

Decades later, a presidential candidate boasted about his pussy-grabbing habit and got elected anyway. I was not entirely surprised, in that I spent the 1990s learning how most cultures — including modern, western cultures — debase females.

Aided by small groups of women singers, I facilitated workshops in 2000 at NELCWIT's Survivors' Project. We shared songs and encouragement with women healing from shame and fear. The work felt more important with each successive news story regarding violence against women.

I wrote the song "Revolution" in 2011 after experiencing harassment from an inebriated man. He approached me in broad daylight as I sat with my six-year-old son, Gillis, on a riverbank and announced that he wanted sex. Jumping up, I swiftly installed my son on the back of our tandem bike and whispered, "Hang on, Honey!" and cycled away from that man as fast as I could.

"We're safe, Honey," I reassured Gillis when we got home. I asked him how he felt.

"That was scary," he answered.

"That man is not well in his head nor in his heart," I told him. "We had to get on the bike and come straight home today. But on another day, we'll go back to the river, maybe with some friends. We have a right to be there."

Satisfied, Gillis ate lunch with me on the porch and later played with his trains. I curled up on the couch and started a new song.

Women:
> I have a right to walk where I please.
> I have a right to be here.
> I shouldn't need to have shaking knees.
> I shouldn't live in cold fear.

Men:
> You have a right to walk where you please.
> You have a right to be here!
> We celebrate your dignity and we won't be part of the problem!
> We will be part of the solution — a human rights revolution!

The whole chorus, in four-part harmony:
> A human rights revolution!

The song ends as women repeat:
> I have a right

and men provide counterpoint:
> I am a man, talking to men.

Rehearsing the new song with Amandla singers over the next few weeks blew the top off emotional stew pots for some, but we stayed with it. Many said the experience brought them deep healing.

I wish I could say that the cycling escape was the last time I had to speak with my son about difficult topics. As he grows, we regularly revisit matters related to misogyny, racism, white privilege, and our culture's addiction to consumption. Parenting is difficult in any era, and ours is no exception. I'm grateful my child grows up in a community unafraid of important questions and discussions.

Freedom songs constitute our soundtrack. When we stumble, we get back on our feet, determined to learn as we go, and we keep singing.

Homeless shelter

Nine Amandla singers stood before me in a tiny, overheated room in February, 2001. Audience members sat in metal folding chairs just inches away, barely outnumbering the singers.

The singers hoped to brighten a winter evening at a shelter for homeless folks housed in the former Northampton fire station. Newly pregnant, I felt queasy due to the building's oppressive heat. Discomfort fell away, however, as folks in the audience smiled, sang along, and clapped. As we wrapped up, I invited them each to find one person they didn't know and say hello for a few moments. People paired up, offering handshakes, conversation, and hugs.

A thin, middle-aged man with grey hair and sunken cheeks approached me shyly. "That last thing you read," he said, timidly. "I like that."

I had read an excerpt from the author Marianne Williamson. "I've got it right here," I told him, sifting through my jumble of sheet music and excerpts. "Here it is." I held it out to him, but he shrank back.

"Can you read that again?" he asked.

"I'd be happy to." I repeated Williamson's words: "There's nothing enlightened about shrinking so that other people won't feel insecure around you. We were born to make manifest the glory of God that is within us. It's not just in some of us; it's in everyone. And as we let our own light shine, we unconsciously give other people permission to do the same."

He looked down, sighing. When he looked up again, he nodded and said, "I like that."

"It's beautiful, isn't it?" I agreed. I introduced myself and asked his name. We shook hands, and I asked, "How are you this evening, Charlie?"

He looked down again. "It's tough," he said. "Glad I got a cot tonight, but . . . I've had some setbacks." We talked until a volunteer appeared in the doorway to let us know the shelter was locking up for the night. It was time for the singers to leave.

Charlie and I walked into the hallway. He paused at a doorway shielded by a curtain. "Is that where you sleep?" I asked. He nodded, pulling the curtain aside to reveal a room filled with cots, blankets, bags, and people. Some of the people sorted through plastic bins. Others sat or lay on cots. Many coughed.

The sight of the large, dim room unnerved me. The Minnesota homeless shelter I'd staffed as a live-in volunteer during the winter of 1986 had been bright and clean with each guest sleeping in a real bed and only two men per room.

Viewing the cot room, I grappled with dueling reactions. *How can they sleep in a room like that?* I wondered. *I'd go crazy!* But I reminded myself that Northampton volunteers worked heroically to shelter desperate people on cold nights. I felt grateful for their efforts.

Why is it even like this? Why do some people have two or more homes while others have none?

I said goodnight to Charlie and offered him the excerpt he liked. He shook his head. "I don't read too good," he admitted.

"Look," I said, taking out a pen. Beneath the printed words, I drew a stick figure, putting a smile on the round face. I added wavy lines that emanated from the figure and finished with a large, shining sun over the scene.

"That's you," I said. "Shining."

I added several more figures and — pointing to myself and to people moving down the hallway — said, "It's all of us. I'd love for you to have this. It's been a pleasure to meet you, Charlie."

He took the piece of paper from my outstretched hand and stared at my elementary rendering. "That's me," he whispered. "It's all of us."

He folded the paper several times and stowed it in his shirt pocket. "Thank you for coming to sing for us." He patted his pocket. "Thanks for telling me the story."

"It's an important story, Charlie," I said, giving him a hug. A kindly volunteer shooed me out the door. I traveled north with friends and arrived at my clean, well-lit apartment.

I brushed my teeth and got into my soft bed. The room was quiet. The temperature was perfect. My possessions were safe. Breakfast ingredients waited for me in cupboards and the fridge. The phone sat on a small table in case I needed help of any kind.

Books. Clean towels. Potted plants.

I snapped on the light and got back up out of bed. I walked to the window and looked at the quiet street below.

I kept hearing the words: "It's not just in some of us; it's in everyone."

Why don't we do it? We don't we refute greed and bring about what we know is right?

I imagined Charlie and all those other people on borrowed cots. I got back into bed and switched off the light.

Growing up in Amandla

I became pregnant with Gillis in 2003, the summer after Amandla's sixteenth season. In light of my five miscarriages, I was determined not to announce too early. When the time seemed right, I shared the joyful news with Amandla members who literally burst into song. I can't imagine better conditions for sharing such news.

For anyone wishing to experience pregnancy filled with bliss and support, I recommend gestating in the company of a choir dedicated to social justice. I pictured my baby developing organs, ligaments, and facial features to the soundtrack of freedom music, love songs, and lullabies from around the world.

My pregnancy sometimes became a topic of discussion when taking Amandla into jails and prisons. I will never forget the connections I made with incarcerated pregnant women, and I'll never stop imagining who and where their children may be today.

Worthy of our children

Eighteen Amandla singers presented three shows for men at the Franklin County Jail in Greenfield. Then we did a very different show for the entire female population incarcerated in the facility at that time: a grand total of four. The limited number made for a very intimate presentation.

We shared passages and quotes about children as we do at nearly every jail show, including one favorite from Pablo Casals: "Let us make the world worthy of its children."

As often happens when we read that passage in public, the women seemed moved by the Casals quote. One woman wrapped herself in her arms and began to rock forward and back.

We sang "Amazing Grace" quietly, and three of the women sang along. The rocking woman, however, stared at the ceiling.

After the song, I said, "Let's take a few minutes to introduce ourselves and chat a bit." Everyone nodded as chatter broke out. I moved toward the rocking woman, who became still and closed her eyes.

Throughout the room, people shook hands, hugged, and traded names. They enjoyed a lot of laughter. I sat next to the young woman who remained tightly wrapped in her arms. "I'm Eveline."

She whispered her name.

"I'm glad to meet you," I said quietly. "How are you doing?"

She began to rock again, then stopped abruptly. "I'm pregnant," she said in a flat voice.

She unwrapped her arms and laid her hands in her lap. I felt torn between kinship and uncertainty about whether it was appropriate to ask personal questions.

"How far along are you?" I asked, hesitantly. "I'm only asking because, you see, I'm pregnant, too."

She twitched and turned toward me. "You are? I'm four months."

Nodding, I said, "Me, too. Due around May 4."

She sighed. "April 30."

I took her hand. I couldn't think of anything else to say. She broke the silence.

"Are you sick in the morning? I threw up every day for a while but it's stopped now," she said wearily.

"I haven't thrown up in this pregnancy," I said, explaining that it was my sixth attempt at becoming a mom.

She drew back, "You lost five?!"

I nodded. She squeezed my hand.

"You want this baby," she said, tenderly.

"Oh, yes," I replied, suddenly weepy. "I'm nearly forty. It feels like my last chance."

"You're twice my age!" she said, smiling.

I replied, "Honey, I'm ancient!" We giggled through tears.

I wanted to ask a hundred questions. What would happen to her? What would happen to her child? What happens to so many of the children for whom we should be making the world worthy?

A prison staff member stepped into the room to let us know that the men, who had to walk a distance from another unit, were on their way.

The Ludlow prison's spacious chapel was nicer than others where we've performed. We planned two shows for that day: one for men, the other for women. There's a lot of waiting in prison, which we've come to expect, so we continued with our vocal warmups.

What we didn't expect was the hooting and hollering that started the moment the guys came through the door. One look at my enormous belly (eight months pregnant), and they broke into loud, confident predictions.

"You got yourself a boy, there, Ma'am!" an older fellow crowed. A younger guy nodded, "Yeah, for sure a boy!" All of the men smiled. Others added similar commentary.

I've learned that it's a gift to share light-hearted banter with people anywhere—even in prisons, homeless shelters, detention centers, and other institutional living situations. I gave it right back to them. "What?! How on earth can you claim to know this child is a boy?" I patted my ballooning belly.

"Everybody can see you're carrying out front, pointy like a football!" a slim fellow exclaimed.

Another chimed in, "You're making a player for the football TEAM!"

Grinning, they high-fived.

With exaggerated haughtiness and stifling a smile, I said, "You guys are full of it! For one thing, my child won't go near a football field only to bruise its precious brain. No way, no thank you." I hammed it up with eye-rolling and hand gestures meant to wave away their nonsense. They ate it up.

"Anyway," I said, "you cannot make such a prediction by looking at the shape of the mother's belly. If this baby is a boy, it won't make you right. It'll make you lucky. Fifty-fifty chance? Big deal!" Everyone laughed.

We played up the running joke throughout the spirited show, which brought to mind a passage from Eduardo Galeano:

> Uruguayan political prisoners may not talk without
> permission or whistle, smile, sing, walk fast, or greet other
> prisoners, nor may they make or receive drawings of pregnant
> women, couples, butterflies, stars, or birds.

I thought, *If this big belly brings joy, it's worth the ribbing!*

Toward the end of the show, a heavy-set man with hair in tightly braided rows set aside joking to say sweetly, "God bless you, Ma'am, and bless that little baby."

Others added to his sentiment as they exited the room with a flurry of encouraging comments.

"You gonna have a beautiful child, Miss."

"You stay safe and blessed. You will be all right."

With twenty minutes to prepare for the women's show, the joviality of the first session left me unprepared for what happened when the women came through the door.

The first woman who entered the chapel took one look at me and said, "Oh, lordy," shaking her head.

The next few women appeared similarly chagrined. Their expressions puzzled me until the seventh or eighth woman entered the chapel. Upon seeing me, she froze and emitted a small cry.

Strikingly beautiful and the color of café au lait, she was every bit as pregnant as I. Her thin frame seemed sapped by the weight of her large belly.

Right behind her came a tall woman with short-cropped hair, no-nonsense and self-confident in a way that set her apart. She stood protectively near the pregnant woman, thus presenting a contrast of vulnerability and strength.

The tall one put her arm around her friend, steering her toward chairs a few rows from the front. "We'll sit here, Honey."

The other women shuffled in and chose seats. They looked at their laps, at each other, or at the singers — anywhere but at my belly.

I held a printed order of songs nearly identical to the one for the men's show. Singers and audience members waited.

I felt dizzy. Instead of starting the first song or doing a standard introduction, I said, "Listen, I'm sorry. I can't pretend there are not two very pregnant women in this room."

The woman who'd entered the room first leaned back in her chair and rolled her eyes. She slapped her thigh. "Thank God," she said sarcastically. "Got that over with!"

Walking a few rows back to stand near the pregnant woman, I said quietly, "I'm due around May fourth. How about you?"

She murmured, "May eighth" and began to cry. The protector hugged her. "It's all right, Baby," she crooned. "Don't you worry."

The young woman covered her face with her hands, saying, "They'll shackle me to the hospital bed when I deliver."

"They will not," said her friend.

"Hell, yeah, they will," retorted the hostile one. "Ask me how I know."

Silence.

I'm not making this any better, I thought. *I should start the singing, but a song can't fix this!*

I battled a rising feeling of panic and couldn't stop myself: "What will happen to your baby?"

Her friend glared at me as the young woman answered mechanically, "Unless a family member takes him, he'll go to foster care. Mama said she'd take him, but she changed her mind." She shuddered. "So he'll just . . . "

"You get twenty minutes with your baby," announced the naysayer with grim satisfaction. "That's all. Then he's gone."

"I'm so sorry," I stammered to the young woman. "I wanted, we wanted to bring you women some comfort, some peace, but I've made it worse, haven't I? Feels like it hardly makes sense to go ahead and sing . . . " My voice trailed off.

I felt like a wild animal, crazy to get out of a cage and feeling more trapped every second.

"No, Ma'am," the protector said firmly. "No, Ma'am. You came to sing. We been looking forward to it all week. So y'all go ahead and sing." Her clear voice brought me back to my senses.

Smiling, the singers nodded. One singer whispered, "Amazing Grace." We followed that song with a quote from James Baldwin: "I imagine one of the reasons people cling to their hates so stubbornly is because they sense, once hate is gone, they will be forced to deal with pain."

We sang "Dimpho Tsarona" from South Africa. The Sotho words mean, "We are bringing our gifts." I shared that Pete Seeger told me of Mahalia Jackson's sentiment: "If you learn a song in another person's language, it's less likely that you'll want to harm them." The women assented with enthusiastic comments.

We sang a few more songs, and I asked for a volunteer from the audience to read a short passage from Helen Keller. A woman with large, beautiful eyes read: "Although the world is very full of suffering, it is also full of the overcoming of it."

She read it quietly, so I asked if she'd read it one more time. She nodded, but no sound came out when she opened her mouth. She swallowed hard and repeated the words in a stronger voice.

A woman a few rows back said, "A-men."

I invited everyone in the room to take a few moments to say hello to someone they'd never met. The singers quickly fanned out in the familiar activity. Soon, the room was abuzz with chatting and laughter, hugs and smiles. Even the snarky woman seemed to enjoy herself. There's simply nothing like one-on-one contact when we go into institutions of any kind.

We introduced "Dios Donde Quiera Esta," an energetic Central American song celebrating how people can recognize the divine in each other. Some of the women joined the refrain: "Alleluia, Gloria Dios!"

I asked one of our basses to recite something Longfellow wrote: "If we could read the secret history of our enemies, we would find in each life a sorrow and a suffering enough to disarm all hostility." One of the few men in the room, his deep voice stood out among sopranos, altos, female tenors, and the incarcerated women.

I hesitated about the next song. "I recently wrote a song about giving birth. Would you like to hear it?" Clapping, they responded in the affirmative.

I added, "It's called 'I Am Opening,' and it's really about giving birth to our dreams, not just to babies. I guess it's about giving birth to ourselves."

The pregnant woman closed her eyes and put her head on her protector's shoulder. We sang: "I am opening, giving birth to my dreams, giving life to my dreams." Many women cried, and a few joined the repeated chant.

After the song, I walked to the end of the row where the pregnant woman sat. I read a passage from Mother Theresa:

> There is a light in this world, a healing spirit more powerful than any darkness we may encounter. We sometimes lose sight of this force when there is suffering, too much pain. Then suddenly the spirit will emerge through the lives of ordinary people who hear a call and answer in extraordinary ways.

The pregnant woman opened her eyes and looked at her protector, who gently and rhythmically patted the younger woman's back.

"Freedom Is Coming" raised the energy and led to a Carl Rowan quote: "It is often easier to become outraged by injustice half a world away, than by oppression a half a block from home."

The women let us know they were right with us. They made many generous comments about loving the music. Thirty minutes before, I had wanted to leave. Now I didn't want it to end.

I chose another upbeat song, "The Storm Is Passin' Over," learned from Ysaye Barnwell of Sweet Honey in the Rock. Some of our favorite material comes from Dr. Barnwell.

One of our tenors read a passage from Merle Shain:

> It is better to light candles than to curse the darkness. It is better to plant seeds than to accuse the earth. The world needs all of our power and love and energy, and each of us has something that we can give. The trick is to find it and use it, to find it and give it away, so there will always be more. We can be lights for each other, and through each other's illumination we will see the way. Each of us is a seed, a silent promise, and it is always spring.

The protector said, "Read that one again, Honey. That was a lot of words, and I think they were all important." After the second time, she nodded and said, "That's very good. Thank you, Honey."

We ended with "You Are A Marvel," words of Pablo Casals I set to music in 2001. I found the words in the autobiography of the great Catalán cellist and peace activist. I especially love his words, "Why should love stop at the border?"

I remembered what one of the prison administrators told me: *Many of these women are here because they were in the wrong place at the wrong time, often in the company of men selling drugs or committing robbery. Many have sold their bodies. Nearly all have been physically or sexually abused. As a result, there's a lot of trauma, mental illness, and addiction.*

As the show ended, I thought about the ubiquitous, undeserved blanket of white privilege so many North Americans live under without realizing it.

A guard came in the door and said, "Time's almost up."

I approached the pregnant woman and asked, "Can I give you a hug?" She nodded, and we embraced belly to belly, our heads forming a peak on an A-frame built around our babies. I could feel kicking but couldn't tell whether it was my baby or hers. I stroked her hair, and it felt like both babies took up kick-boxing. Maybe they were trying to hug, too?

Others stood, their eyes glued to the scene. I did not want to let her go, but another reminder from a guard nudged me. "I'll be thinking about you every day," I whispered. The protector smiled and pulled her friend away.

The snarky one stood off to the side as if the rules were different for her and she could stay in the chapel if she felt like it. I approached her. She refused to look at my face. Her eyes focused on my belly and she coughed once.

"Thank you for coming," I said. She ignored me. Desperate emotion rolled through me and I grabbed her hand. She wouldn't look me in the eye, but she didn't pull her hand away. Holding her hand firmly, I said, "I want you to know I'll be thinking about you."

Never did she raise her eyes from my belly, but just before she left, she squeezed my hand.

The Amandla singers walked out into the sunshine on that April Saturday. For me, it's always astonishing to leave a prison, to stand in a parking lot and put my hand on a car handle, knowing I can open it and climb inside.

Also on a Saturday, six weeks later, my son emerged into a world where he was wanted, loved, and afforded many privileges simply because of who he is and what he looks like.

Since then, every Saturday, I ask Gillis, "Guess what?"

He smiles and asks, "What?" even though he knows what comes next.

I say, "Today is Saturday. You were born on a Saturday, and that was the best day ever. And now every day is the best day, because I get to be your mama."

Even in his early teens, he still snuggles into me when I say it. Sometimes he says, "Oh, Mama, I know." Someday, he'll probably ask me to knock it off. For now, I glory in our Saturday morning ritual.

Each Saturday, I also think about another child my son's age. That baby's Mama was so beautiful with her big belly and so sad with uncertainty and fear.

As I move about in freedom and privilege to watch my son grow, leap, play and learn, I think: *It can be better. We could guarantee what Gillis has for every child. It's not out of our reach as a society, and we have to make it happen.*

When the baseball bug bit Gillis, it bit hard despite the fact that when his dad took him to the first T-ball practice, it didn't go well. "They were mean to me," my seven-year-old reported upon returning home.

"Really?" I asked. "In what way?"

"They say boys shouldn't wear pink," he replied with disgust, "and boys shouldn't have long hair. They laughed and called me names." After a moment's pause, he added, "I'm never wearing pink outside of our house again."

It was bound to happen some time, I thought. Still, my heart sank in the wake of my son's first real cultural bruising. "Oh, Honey,"

I soothed. "I hope those kids learn to accept a variety of styles. They sound a bit narrow-minded. I'm sorry they teased you."

"The kids?" Gillis retorted with an incredulous expression. "It wasn't the kids. It was the coaches. They're mean."

I inhaled deeply, releasing the air slowly. I knew my kid would need to learn to face his own battles. It was he, not I, who chose pink stretchy pants as his favorites. He also chose to wear them inside out because "the seams feel yucky." In fact, he wore all of his clothes, except for jackets and footwear, inside out for about four years. Some people felt the need to comment on the practice. Whatever.

Gillis didn't want his hair cut, and I saw no reason to shear my child in order to conform to a dictum regarding "what boys should look like."

I suppose I should have issued a warning before sending him off to face the wolves for the first time. Oh, well. I took a test to get my driver's license but not to become a parent. Most of the time, I just wing it.

After his fourth T-ball practice, Gillis announced, "It's time to cut my hair."

I attempted to keep my face expressionless. *Score one for mainstream culture.* I tried to sound cheerful as I stroked the strawberry blond locks reaching halfway down his back. "If that's what you want, Sweetie, sure. How much do you want cut off?"

He demonstrated with his thumb and forefinger: about two inches. Minus two inches, his tresses no doubt still struck his tormenters as too girly, but Gillis never mentioned it again.

His boycott of pink lasted about seven years. A few months before his fourteenth birthday, while shopping at Salvation Army Half-Price Wednesday, Gillis held up a pink button-down shirt. "This is a cool color," he said. "Can I get it? It's half of $2.99." I nodded, smiling.

I took my little victory dance into the next aisle where no one could see me.

In the intervening years between T-ball masculinity boot camp and the onset of adolescence, Gillis became increasingly enthralled with all things baseball. I wondered if it could be genetic—perhaps he channeled my dad, the grandfather he never met. Dad adored listening to our Montreal Expos on the transistor radio as he tended his garden. "Hot Dog!" meant the Expos scored a run. "Dad Gummit!" let us know the other team took the lead.

On my fifth birthday, Daddy hinted that a surprise awaited me. "Get in the car," he said with a grin. "It's just you and me today." I couldn't believe it. In our busy family, I never got time with just Daddy. As we approached Montreal's Jarry Park, I figured out the surprise. We were going to a real, live Expos game.

Gillis continues in the same besotted tradition. Rather than worshipping the defunct Expos, however, his is the Church of Red Sox. He displays ardent devotion by hanging pennants and posters, listening to every game on the radio, recording statistics in a little notebook, and making a pilgrimage to Fenway Park each summer with his dad. Left to his own devices, Gillis's dad would skip it but nevertheless agrees to abet our child's mania.

When Gillis was nine, I read a newspaper article about a local author named Richard Andersen. "Check this out, Bunster," I called to Gillis. "A guy who lives in Montague wrote a book about baseball." Montague is about ten miles from Greenfield.

Gillis left his train set and peered over my shoulder. "Is it about the Red Sox?" he asked.

"No," I said, "it's a great story about a 1934 team from Springfield. They had an African-American player nicknamed Bunny, and when they traveled to North Carolina to play in

eastern championships, the other team refused to play unless
Bunny stayed off the field. The Springfield team captain, Tony,
said he wouldn't play unless the other team welcomed Bunny,
and the rest of the team followed suit. They ended up coming
home without playing."

Springfield is about forty miles from Greenfield.

Gillis whistled. "Wow," he said. "The championships.
Unbelievable."

"Which part do you find unbelievable?" I asked. "That they
refused to play, or that the other team refused to accept Bunny?"

Gillis shook his head. "All of it," he said. "It's crazy."

I showed him the author's photo. "Let's get in touch with this
guy," I suggested. "What a sweet face. Sounds like he did tons of
research. You love baseball, and I love history. Let's write him a
letter. He lives nearby and teaches writing at Springfield College."

Richard's warm response led to a beautiful friendship
as well as an invitation for Amandla to sing at a Springfield
College event on February 9, 2014 to celebrate the publication of
A Home Run for Bunny. We also met the book's illustrator, Gerald
Purnell, a lovely man.

Richard met me at the art gallery's entrance. "Tony King is on
his way," he announced gleefully.

"Tony K—" I gasped. "The team captain from the story?"

"That's the one," said Richard, smiling. "At ninety-six, he's
the only one left."

As I gathered the Amandla singers to begin our short set, I
whispered to Gillis, "Guess who's coming?"

"Who?" he asked, eying the snack table and trying to take in
the hubbub of yet another gig with Mommy.

"Tony. King."

Gillis froze. His hands floated to his mouth. "The captain?" he
whispered.

Anthony "Tony" King signs A Home Run for Bunny *by Springfield College professor Richard Andersen.*

I nodded. He scanned the room with wild swings of his head. I took his hand. "He's not here yet, Sweetie, but when he comes, you'll get to shake hands with a real-life hero."

"He was a champion," Gillis said dreamily.

"In more ways than one," I confirmed.

Photos from that day show Gillis with a star-struck expression. Once Tony arrived, Gillis remained at his side and took his eyes off our hero for only one moment: when the chocolate cake appeared on the reception table. After that, he resumed his position near Tony. My child beamed when Tony signed our copy of the book. With chocolate frosting rimming his lips, Gillis stayed very close to that powerful man who stood up for what is right.

A few days after the gallery event, a package from Richard arrived in the mail addressed to Gillis. It had curious heft. My son tore off the wrapping to find a baseball signed by Tony King.

Gillis carried it around for days, even sleeping with it. He decided to keep it in an acrylic display case, right under the spot where the book jacket from *A Home Run For Bunny* hangs on his wall.

Every kid needs real-life heroes, and it's a blessing to discover heroes close to home.

the Education of a reSister

I lay in the grass on an uncharacteristically quiet afternoon in 1975. I heard no lawn mowers, no pesky brothers, no list of chores announced by Mom. Just birdsong and rustling leaves punctuated by screen doors slamming. Mesmerized by puffy white clouds, I let my mind wander in a rare moment of peace.

I was eleven.

I dozed, then opened my eyes. Something moved across my field of vision. The dark lines of an Air Force jet made the clouds look even whiter and softer.

I recalled a boy at school bragging that planes taking off from Plattsburgh's Strategic Air Command Base could carry and drop nuclear bombs. Anthony announced the fact during a boastful rant about planning to join the Civil Air Patrol. His family lived on the air base. Anthony told me that his cat, Napoleon, loved cheese. He also told me his family moved a lot. He impressed me with the list of places he'd lived, including tropical countries.

He claimed to know the number of bombs housed at the base near our school and recited in an authoritative voice the cost of building and maintaining each jet.

I had pondered such large numbers only when Daddy urged me to peer through our telescope. The cost of military hardware brought to mind the number of stars in the sky.

During my peaceful afternoon on the side lawn, several other military planes followed the first. *Where do they get the money, I wondered, to buy such expensive planes? How do they pay the bomb makers?*

Unaware of taxation, the Pentagon, or defense budgets, I struggled to figure it out. I earned a few dollars as a mother's helper and sometimes subbed on my eldest brother's paper route, but I couldn't imagine how flying planes around in the sky and storing bombs generated income.

Eveline's first attempt at political organizing took place in April, 1983, when she and fellow student Troy Oechsner spent months planning a march and rally against the nuclear arms race during nationwide activity endorsing a nuclear freeze. The march took the activists down Plattsburgh's Broad Street. In the background: St. John's Church, where Eveline spent many hours of Catholic childhood.

Then I remembered the fines. On rare occasions when I kept library books past due dates, I paid a few pennies. I asked the librarian if the money went to buy new books. She smiled, saying, "It's a little more complicated than that. We're supported by the overall town budget. But yes, some of the pennies help buy new books."

I love librarians, I thought. *They're so smart.*

An epiphany shattered my reverie and I sat up with a start. *The air base is in our town. If it's one big budget, maybe library fines help pay for planes and bombs! A lot of people forget to return books on time.*

I generally tried to remain quiet in our town about the fact that I didn't share the fervor and loyalty many locals felt toward the air base. I secretly wished it didn't exist. The thought of expensive planes dropping bombs made me angry because I knew that bombs hurt people, animals, trees, and rivers.

It's so stupid, I thought.

Following my so-called epiphany, I resolved never again to keep a library book past the due date. *I won't pay for stuff like bombs and weapons,* I promised myself.

I told no one. I don't know if my family noticed my new campaign of obsessively checking due dates of the many library books in our household.

The topic of nuclear bombs came up at school, and I learned that we had nukes because the Soviets had nukes. I learned that the Soviet Union used to be called Russia and went mad with hunger for dangerous weaponry, leading to sensible Americans having no choice but to join the Arms Race.

I suspected it was more complicated, but still considered it stupid to build and buy bombs we should definitely never use. Still, I knew I'd be called unpatriotic if I admitted my true feelings, so I went undercover, saying the pledge and singing the national anthem in our military town, though I felt resistant all the while.

Three years later, Marcel and Judy, a courageous young couple with two small children, stood up in church one Sunday to announce their refusal to pay federal income taxes because the vast percentage paid for war. This went against their convictions. The explanation from a faith perspective affirmed my feelings and at age fourteen, I knew my path.

Within a few years, I began publicly protesting the arms race.

Beach play

The boys roughhoused at the edge of Lake Champlain. I decided to make a sand castle.

Seven years old, I worked alone until I noticed a girl about my age watching me.

She asked, "Can I help?"

I nodded, happy to gain a buddy. We set about adding to the creation and dug an elaborate moat. We worked steadily, chatting away.

One of my brothers called to me from the water. Daddy prepared to send him flying through the air in a grand dive.

I'd seen the trick a hundred times, but it always impressed me. I paused to watch its completion. Gloating, I said, "That's my brother and my daddy. It's a great trick, isn't it?"

"That's your daddy?" she asked, narrowing her eyes.

"Yes," I said proudly.

"Your daddy looks like an Injun," she said, her voice hard and cold. I shivered despite the noonday sun.

"My daddy's Scottish, English, and German," I told her.

"He looks dark to me. He doesn't have hair no place but his head," she said, as if proving a point. "Normal men have hair on their chests and under their arms. Normal men have light skin."

"What?" I shouted. "My daddy is a normal man. Shut up."

I knew that saying "Shut up" was forbidden, but I felt very angry.

I felt tempted to assure her that my daddy was not this dark all year, that it happened only during the summer. But I suspected she would somehow use my reasoning against me. Instead, I said, "Go build your own sand castle, Stupid."

"Good," she said. "I don't want to play with you anymore. You stink, dirty Injun."

She huffed away. I was pretty sure we had no Indian relatives, but the exchange left me feeling deeply sad.

I recalled a television advertisement depicting a stately Native American figure emerging on horseback from a forest into a trash-filled clearing next to a highway. The ad ended with a single tear rolling down the majestic man's cheek. The ad impressed me deeply, as did my parents' frequent reminders that all people are related. I knew the girl was just being a jerk. I finished the sand castle on my own.

Not until I was an adult did I learn that the man who portrayed the so-called crying Indian wasn't a Native American but rather was an Italian-American. My introduction to the ugly truths about violence done to Native Americans began that day on the beach when that unfortunate child, no doubt echoing bigoted adults, shot off her mouth.

Bigotry 101

Teachers announced the end of recess. As usual, I dawdled, one of the last to leave the playground. In grade school, I felt that hard chairs and ticking clocks proved no contest compared with clouds and trees.

I moved absent-mindedly toward the school when a shove from behind forced me to the ground. I tasted dirt as a snicker from above caused my stomach to flip-flop. *I didn't even see him out here! I thought he was absent today.* Panicking, I wondered, *Why does he hate me so much?*

Turning my head to confirm my tormenter's identity, I closed my eyes in time to avoid a dirt spray sent up by the toe of his shoe.

Glancing toward the school, I prayed, *Please help. Anybody!* But the spiteful boy and I were just out of sight of the windows.

I braced for more physical attacks, but none came. Instead, he lowered his face to mine and hissed, "You frogs are the [plural n-word] of Canada. Why don't you go back across the border, you moron?"

I knew "frogs" represented slander against French-speaking people of Québec. But I didn't know the other word, "[n-word]" Satisfied for the moment, the bully ran into the building. I repeated the new word under my breath and filed it away.

Reprimanded for daydreaming in class, my face grew hot. I couldn't wait to get home. I had to ask Daddy about the new word.

I hesitated at his workshop door. I watched Daddy make oboe reeds before dinnertime. I had to ask someone, and I sure couldn't ask Mama. Any question referring to the word "frog" would distress my sensitive, immigrant mother.

"Daddy?" I stood just inside the door.

"Mm-hmm?" He didn't take his eyes off the red thread and cork, ingredients of reed-making.

"Daddy?" I said again, trying to get his attention.

"Yes, Duck-Duck," he said absently.

"Daddy, what's a [n-word]?"

With a scowl, he lowered the reeds to his lap. I regretted the question. But instead of snapping, he pushed his project away and turned on his stool.

"Come here, Duck-Duck," he said gently, lifting me to his lap. I was stunned that my question succeeded in getting my father's complete attention, not an easy task.

"Where did you hear that word?" he asked quietly.

I balked, knowing it went against code to tattle on another kid. I hadn't told a soul about the bullying that whole school year. No one bothered to ask even after my two trips to the hospital with intense stomach pains.

"Schwet-schwet?" said Daddy, using a nickname he learned while living in Germany. "Where did you hear that hateful word?"

I related an abridged version, judiciously omitting accounts of ongoing abuse. "A stupid kid said us frogs are the [plural n-word] of Canada."

Daddy's eyes widened. "I see," he said firmly. He sounded angry, but I could tell he wasn't angry with me. He held me tenderly, and I began to feel safer than I had in a long time.

"Honey, I need to talk with you about ignorance."

Oh, boy: another new word. "Where are they?" I asked. "Do they live in hills, like the ones near our sidewalk?"

*Eveline's brother Andrew
and four-year-old
Eveline in 1968*

"Live in hills? Who?" my father asked, puzzled.

"The ants."

A lifelong punster, my father chuckled as he realized I'd heard "ants" in the word "ignorance."

He explained, "Fear makes some people hate others for ridiculous reasons. You know how Uncle Vince has skin that's darker than yours and mine?"

I nodded, warmed by the thought of my father's best friend who visited from New Jersey each summer. We all loved Uncle Vince.

"Some confused people don't like Uncle Vince because of his skin color."

"What!? Why?" I demanded, astonished and outraged that anyone could dislike Uncle Vince. *Who can resist a tuba player?*

"Ignore-ANTS!" Daddy said, chuckling again. Growing serious, he said, "That kid told you a lie. French-Canadians are not worth less than other people. Too bad he doesn't understand that French-Canadians are hardworking, fun-loving, and generous. You know that and I know that."

Daddy fell head-over-heels in love not only with Mama but with her enormous, rollicking family, as well.

"That brat is in crummy company with anyone who uses the n-word to try to feel superior. Ignorant people put others down for the color of their skin or because of where they come from. In this case, Québec."

"That's really stupid," I said. "We're great!" Giggling, I added, "We're so great, we even like you, even though you're not froggy at all!"

Those sweet moments with Daddy helped dispel the troubled boy's power over me. I watched my back more carefully on the playground after that, but I must have exuded more confidence because, gradually, that twisted young soul stopped taunting me. Perhaps a new glint in my eye suggested he shouldn't mess with me. Or maybe he got bored and moved on to new victims.

On her seventh birthday in 1971, Eveline rides her brand new bike.

That day, I learned new words and important lessons. I knew instinctively that no human was either a frog or a [n-word]. A small flame kindled inside of me. I knew the world could be more kind, and that people could be less scared.

Right to life

Soon after the 1973 US Supreme Court decision Roe v. Wade led to abortion legalization, an item appeared in the Saint John's Church bulletin encouraging parishioners to attend a rally sponsored by Champlain Valley Right to Life. A doctor's wife cornered my mother after mass, urging her to attend. "Bring the girl," she said. With steely eyes trained on me, the woman added, "You can't start too early teaching a girl what's right in the eyes of God." I was nine.

Mom seemed unenthusiastic. But she felt obliged to put in an appearance, given her status as an immigrant in a community where people routinely looked down on French Canadians.

The next Saturday, we headed southwest from Plattsburgh to an isolated spot in the village of Schuyler Falls where a new abortion clinic operated. Mom said little during the twenty-minute ride. I had no idea what to expect. When we arrived, I saw that the clinic, a renovated older home, looked small and common.

Protesters milled about as Mom parked the car along the country road. Coffee, muffins, and brochures covered a card table. As the only child there, I deduced that no other girls would learn "what's right in the eyes of God." Rather than feeling sanctimonious, I felt lonely and out of place.

I nibbled a tasteless muffin. Its appeal decreased further when I saw a large poster propped against the side of the card table. The poster, nearly as tall as I, showed body parts thrown into a bag-lined trash pail. I could make out tiny feet and hands. A gag reflex propelled me down the road where I deposited the rest of the muffin behind a tree.

The steely-eyed woman from church picked up a megaphone and issued instructions. "The cars usually arrive around ten o'clock. Please be prepared to display a poster, join in prayers, and make our presence known."

Protestors gathered materials as the woman sang hymns through the megaphone, making the songs sound eerie. From then on, I thought of her as the megaphone lady. People stomped their feet in the morning chill. A few sang along weakly.

"Here they come!" someone cried.

Megaphone Lady began shouting a prayer familiar to me from rosary recitations, "Hail Mary, full of grace, the Lord is with thee. Blessed art thou amongst women, and blessed is the fruit of thy womb, Jesus." Instead of continuing with the prayer, though, she yelled, "Fruit of thy womb! Fruit of thy womb!" over and over as two dark sedans slid by with three or four young women in each car.

A couple of protesters made moves to run down the driveway after the cars but were told, "No, no, we can't go past here." I heard muttered phrases that sounded angry and threatening.

Protestors sympathized with each other about what they'd like to do in order to "show those harlots the errors of their ways."

I heard my mother explain in a polite voice that she was due to pick up a child at swim class. I was unaware of anyone in my family having swim class that morning but hid my surprise at the possibility that my mother had fibbed. I just wanted to go home. If we left earlier than the other protestors, that was fine with me.

After mass the next day, Mom received accolades for showing up at the protest. My heart sank, however, when the megaphone lady extracted a commitment for another appearance the following week.

The second protest went about the same as the first. Both times, I couldn't read my mother's expression on the way home. She seemed preoccupied.

On the third Saturday, I tried to come up with an excuse so I could stay home or at least convince my mom that the boys should come, too.

"No, Eveline," Mom said wearily. "This isn't a subject for boys. It's for girls. You need to know how dangerous it can be when . . . when you're older and it's time to be . . . careful."

I didn't know what I would want to be careful about, but I went along because Mom seemed sad.

The megaphone lady appeared in rare form when we arrived. The group of protesters, more numerous than before, spoke excitedly in quick whispers. Something felt different.

Megaphone Lady approached Mom and me. "We're going to stop them this time," she said firmly. "The murderers must not be permitted to enter that house of evil."

Letting her words sink in for a moment, she continued. "God wants us to use our bodies to protect those babies. When the cars come, we'll block the entrance to the driveway. It may be against man's law, but we're in accordance with God's law."

Leaning down to grip my upper arms with her hands, she breathed right into my face. "You," she said. "You have a special role. You must stand your ground. Don't move an inch, no matter what. Do you hear me? God wants you to stand fast. You are a soldier of God."

Megaphone Lady terrified me. Her hands felt like claws on my arms, even through my jacket.

My mother made a small, indistinct sound. Looking at Mom's face, I saw she'd lost her redheaded glow. Her face looked like a blank sheet of paper.

I heard a shout. "They're coming!"

Megaphone Lady dragged me with her. Protesters quickly formed a line four or five people deep across the road. The cars moved slowly toward us. I could see the driver of the first car, a man with a dark beard. His eyes widened as he approached the blockade. Looking in his rearview mirror, he made an exaggerated shrugging motion, perhaps to signal bewilderment to the driver of the second car.

Megaphone Lady began to bellow a song. Ruining one of my favorite songs by sending it through her device with a toxic voice, she croaked, "Let there be peace on earth, and let it begin with me."

For a second, I almost began to laugh. This woman struck me as one of the least peaceful people I'd ever met. Then I grew angry. I wondered how long it would take me to walk ten miles home. I must have stepped to one side. Instantly, her God-loving, peaceful claw was on me once more, ordering me to remain in place.

The cars crept toward us. The driver shook his head rapidly and seemed to yell something, but I couldn't hear him because the windows were closed. I noticed tears streaming down the face of the woman in the front passenger seat. She covered her face but peeked through her fingers as the cars advanced by inches.

The first car was about one foot from me. It kept coming until I felt hands stronger than the claws. My mother yanked me from the grip of Megaphone Lady, yelling, "Come on, Eveline. We're going home!"

As Mom pulled me away, I saw the protesters, including Megaphone Lady, scatter as they ran from the cars. *Wow*, I thought. *She told me to stand my ground for God, but now she's running away. What a jerk.*

Yet she continued to bellow her song, punctuated by shouts of "Murderers! Murderers!"

I looked back to see the second car slide by with weeping young women inside. A dark-haired woman sitting behind the driver looked right at me and shook her head, mouthing one word three times. "Sorry. Sorry. Sorry."

Mom and I never went back. If she regretted falling out with the church's inner circle, she did not speak of it.

Over the years, I've heard many sides of the abortion debate. While I love babies and honor life, I believe that each woman must decide for herself what happens with her reproductive organs, her body, her life.

My reluctant visits to Schuyler Falls terrified me. Yet I gleaned important lessons from the experience. I learned about judgment, hypocrisy, and double standards from members of Champlain Valley Right to Life. I learned about people interpreting God's will to fit their own agenda.

It occurred to me, years later, that my injury or death under the wheel of a car would have represented a coup for Megaphone Lady. I suspect she felt willing to sacrifice a nine-year-old child in the service of her cause.

After Mom and I stopped going to the protests, the Schuyler Falls clinic closed down temporarily after a fire, giving me the opportunity to learn a new word: arson.

In a dream, I travel back to that dreaded spot. This time, however, I have an adult's sensibilities. I take the leader aside, laying her megaphone on the card table. "Listen," I say, "talk to me about the evils of abortion after you adopt twenty or thirty children. Get on your high horse after you turn your second home over to people who live under bridges. Quote God after you read the Gospels in full. Oh, and stop ruining my favorite songs."

My real dream, however, is that education about sex, birth control, and women's rights leads to a decrease in unwanted pregnancies. An abortion is not a walk in the park. But neither is parenting while living in poverty. No woman should have to carry a pregnancy resulting from any form of coercion. There are many forms of violence, including marriages or relationships that feel like prisons. A woman must have the right to choose.

Tiptoeing out of Mass

When I was twelve, the bishop delivered a special message at Saint John's, the large Catholic church where my family attended mass. Church ladies planned a luncheon in his honor. Preparations sent the parish into a frenzy for weeks. Of course, we wore our very best to mass that day.

The place was packed. We got no special treatment when it came to seating, even though Daddy was the choir director. Though arriving early, we could find seats only toward the very back, which proved a stroke of luck for me.

The bishop began his remarks. I concentrated on his outlandish headgear and settled in for supreme boredom. He droned on as my mind wandered, but I snapped to attention when I heard him say, "Birth control."

I read about many things at the library, including birth control, which I knew was against the rules for Catholics. But I'd never heard an adult say the words out loud, much less a high-ranking clergyman. But the bishop said it several times: birth control.

I listened more closely. Now he talked about women, never mentioning men. He spoke of women in foreign countries and women "here at home." I tried to follow his thread as he mentioned God's will, the sanctity of marriage, and the miracle of

At Eveline's first communion party in 1971, her youngest brother, Ian, stands in front, and her middle brother, Robert, comforted by their mother, wears the blue jumper. Her eldest brother, Andrew, served as altar boy at the ceremony. The rest of the folks are mostly family members from Québec.

babies. That sounded fine, but soon the bishop made it sound like every evil in the world was due to women's selfishness. There was much I didn't understand about sex and relationships, but I knew that the bishop was full of it.

Feeling hot and angry, I breathed in shallow patterns. The bishop's words suffocated me. My three brothers seemed unaffected. They weren't even listening. I turned to look at Mom sitting next to me. She patted my hand and looked into my eyes without smiling.

Something big shifted in me. "Mom," I whispered fiercely. "I'm going outside."

Instead of shaking her head or hissing that I should stay right in my seat, Mom looked resigned. Her mouth in a thin line, she glanced at the bishop and looked again at me. Squeezing my hand, she whispered, "Alright, Eveline."

I couldn't believe it. I'd never left mass before. I tiptoed to the back door. I looked back toward the pews. People sitting in front of my family didn't realize I had exited, but the few sitting behind us whispered and shook their heads. As if made of wood, my mother stared toward the front.

I sat on the stone steps and listened to the muffled sounds of singing, bells, and shuffling feet. The heavy wooden doors may well have been three miles thick for all the closeness I felt to my fellow Catholics. I considered walking the short distance home but felt too drained.

The bells began to peal. I knew the big doors would soon swing open and parishioners would stream out on their way to the luncheon. I sprang from the stone steps and eased into thick bushes. People chatted, oblivious to the deserter in their midst.

Finally, I saw through the leaves that my family descended the steps. Mom looked around. I stepped from the bushes and said, "Can we go home?"

She surprised me again, saying, "Yes, let's go home." No one said anything in the car. I felt guilty for ruining everyone's special Sunday.

At home, I took off my shiny black shoes. I knew I must find Mom and tell her my decision. I approached her with dread, wanting to get it over with but knowing my words would make my mother very sad.

"I'm not going back there, Mom," I said. She continued making sandwiches. In a small voice, I added, "The bishop is wrong. What he said about women is not true."

Mom laid the butter knife in the cap of the mayonnaise jar. She spoke haltingly, "What the church fathers say is tradition. They have to, they must protect the church. They . . ." She was out of words, but I felt a huge lecture coming on.

Mom surprised me once more. "You have to make your own decision, Eveline. You must act in faith. I pray you never lose your faith. It's the greatest gift we have, a gift from God."

I walked to my bedroom, closing the door. My catechism class prepared for confirmation the next year. But my deeply devout mother said it was my decision? I felt scared. I didn't want the bishop's words anywhere near me, but I wanted my mother to tell me what to do. The stark shift in maternal policy left me confused.

I took my mother at her word, accepting one of the greatest gifts she ever gave me. *She says I can choose. I reject words and ideas that suffocate me.*

There were several Catholic churches in Plattsburgh. My best friend, Cassie, introduced me to the John XXIII Newman Center, a small church with modern architecture located across the street from the university. The priest, Father Dan Keefe, had legions of fans due to his kindness and understanding. He seemed like a regular person instead of a removed, disapproving judge. Filled with compassion, humor, and down-to-earth wisdom, he became a true friend. At the Newman Center, I found a spiritual home that allowed me to remain in the Catholic Church for a few more years.

After leaving Plattsburgh as a young adult, my spirituality never again fit into a specific church or belief system. I tiptoed out of mass at the age of twelve and continued to grow and change.

At nineteen, I drove across this big country with two friends. My mind blew wide open during my first major road trip as I heard different accents, ate regional foods, and stood on the Continental Divide. When we stopped for gas in Montana, the sight of the big sky seized my heart. *I could stay here forever. I could stow away in a barn until I work up the courage to ask a farmer for work. I'm strong and I know farm work. There's so much space here!*

One of my friends finished pumping gas and handed me the keys. "Your turn," she said. "I'm sleeping in back."

Upon returning east, I stopped at my tiny basement apartment in the hospital district of Albany, New York, but didn't stay long. The time had come to hit the road again, but with a different purpose.

Traveling with a friend I hadn't seen in awhile, I hitchhiked north to Plattsburgh. The excitement of my big trip wore off as I imagined my weary parents listening to tales of my adventures.

My parents loved to travel when they could afford it, but I knew their journeys at the time consisted of trips to the hospital and back due to my father's illness. Cancer was their co-pilot and navigator.

During my cross-country trip, I missed Thanksgiving with my family. So did my dad, confined to the hospital for a few days. The mood at home would be tense and sad. I longed for Montana.

I returned to the present when my friend exclaimed, "A ride!" Young women traveling together for safety, we hopped into the cab of an eighteen-wheeler.

The wizened French-Canadian truck driver put our backpacks behind the seats and regaled us with tales of the road. He conveyed us safely to our destination and wagged his finger as we jumped to the ground. "Don't take rides with creeps. I got some kids, too. Stay safe and don't break your parents' hearts!"

My pal headed off to find her boyfriend. Slowly, I walked to my parents' small home.

Mom was in the kitchen preparing dinner in customary efficient bursts between teaching piano lessons. Dad was in their bedroom tapping away at a manual typewriter.

"How you doing, Dad?" I asked, giving him a half-hug. He was so thin. I feared he would break in two if I hugged him like I used to before he got sick.

"I'm OK," he said. "I'm working on a history of the Seventh Army Symphony. There are so many great stories about our travels throughout Europe!"

"I can't wait to read it," I said. I recalled with fondness when, in 1977, my father organized a large reunion in Washington, DC to celebrate the twenty-fifth anniversary of the Seventh Army

Symphony Orchestra. I was twelve when my family traveled to our nation's capital. We visited monuments and museums that filled me with thrilling pride, and I enjoyed meeting brilliant musicians, longtime friends of my dad's.

"Good to see you, Dad. I'm back from my trip," I said in a low voice. Just as I didn't want to hug him too hard, I didn't want to speak too loudly. He turned from his typewriter with a smile, and I saw that his cheekbones were very prominent. I found it difficult to look at him.

"We loved your postcards!" he said, his eyes lighting up.

I wanted to tell him about the Grand Canyon, seeing the Pacific Ocean for the first time, and riding streetcars in San Francisco, but felt hesitant. Mom interrupted my awkwardness, announcing to the household, "One more lesson, then dinner!"

Gesturing with my head toward the kitchen, I smiled. "She doesn't stay in one spot for long."

My mother raised four children and acted as guardian for a niece. She taught piano and French lessons and occasionally worked as a translator. Mom could zip to the courthouse to translate for a proceeding, rush home to take someone to the doctor or dentist, and then back home to teach more lessons.

Dad's employment days were behind him. Cancer nibbled his thin body. For years, he taught music in public schools and held the post of principal oboist for the Vermont Symphony, just across Lake Champlain. Now, just sitting up and typing drained him.

"She moves fast enough for both of us," sighed Dad. "I wish this wasn't so hard on her. I can handle the pain, but she's the one who's really suffering."

Stories of my trip dissipated like smoke. I hated myself for being so selfish, but I wanted to tell just one story — any story — about my adventures. But I didn't, because given what everyone at home was dealing with, it seemed insensitive.

Instead, I asked, "Was it OK at the hospital?"

Dad rubbed his knees. "Oh, yes. They're very good. They took fluid from my lungs."

We sat in fading daylight, listening to muffled sounds of piano. I stood and kissed the top of my father's head. "I'm going to help with dinner or something."

"Thanks for coming home, Honey," Dad said. "We missed you."

After dinner, Mom and I washed and dried dishes as my brothers—twenty-two, sixteen, and thirteen—disappeared into their rooms. I sighed heavily.

Mom said, "Thanks for telling us a little bit about your trip. You don't seem too excited about it, though."

Swallowing hard, I said, "How can I be excited when I see what you're dealing with? I feel guilty for going across the country and having fun!"

Mom's hands stopped moving in dishwater. Her shoulders sagged. *I'm making it worse,* I thought.

Mom straightened to her full height, just over five feet. She said, "Tomorrow is Saturday. I don't teach until ten o'clock. You and I will go somewhere special after breakfast. I want to show you something."

I dried a dinner plate and asked, "Where are we going?"

"You'll see," Mom answered.

Early the next morning, Mom handed me a bulging plastic bag. It was full of clothes. Pointing to the car, Mom said, "Put it in the back seat, please."

Mom drove down Cornelia and parked on Clinton Street, which is a couple of short blocks crowded with small shops and offices. The buildings are mostly three stories with apartments on upper floors.

I stayed in the car for a moment after Mom got out. I wondered about a bag of clothes and a section of town where college kids and low-income folks rent seedy apartments.

"Do you know someone who lives here?" I asked, hesitantly stepping from the car. Mom motioned for me to bring the bag from the back seat. I grabbed it and followed her to a beat-up door.

"I know several people," she said over her shoulder. "I want you to meet them."

We climbed two flights of dimly lit stairs. I wrinkled my nose at the smell of old cigarette smoke and older urine.

Mom knocked on a door and called "Bonjour!" I heard voices from inside. The door swung open. A tall, beautiful woman with very dark skin and stunningly white teeth exclaimed, "Madame Céline! Bonjour! Bienvenue!"

In a gesture familiar to my French-speaking family, the two women kissed each other lightly on both cheeks. Mom motioned that I should follow her into the dingy apartment. I clutched the plastic bag and went in.

The floor was nearly covered with mattresses. A small, battered table stood against a wall with three straight-backed chairs. In addition to the tall woman, there was one other woman plus seven children.

"Asseyez-vous, s'il vous plaît!" the tall woman said with a smile. She dusted two of the chairs with a paper napkin before we took our seats.

"C'est ma fille, Eveline," Mom said, introducing me. "Eveline, Sareeya."

The woman and I shook hands.

"Enchantée," Sareeya said with utmost grace.

I mumbled, "Bonjour, Madame."

Gorgeous, healthy-looking children peered at us. The other adult, however, sat on a mattress with her back against a wall. She stared into space.

"Elle est fatiguée aujourd'hui," the tall woman said gently, explaining that the woman on the mattress was tired that day. A look passed between Mom and Sareeya, signaling shared understanding that the woman's fatigue was not limited to one day.

"Bonjour, Nadia!" Mom said gently. "Comment ça va, mon amie?"

Nadia lifted her head a couple of inches without changing her expression.

Sareeya brought us water in two plastic cups. Slicing an apple, she set pieces on a plate. She gave us paper napkins and settled into the third chair.

Mom explained that the bag contained requested items for the children. Rattling off names, Mom pulled clothing from the bag, holding up shirts and pants for each child except the baby. Then, from the bottom of the bag, Mom produced a package of disposable diapers. Sareeya smiled.

I had never seen my mother touch a disposable diaper. I surveyed the room while trying not to appear nosy. Chatter faded into the background as a wild monologue ran in my head.

How can people live like this? What's wrong with Nadia? Is she the mother of some of these kids? How can Sareeya be so serene and gracious? Where are the men? What will happen to these people? I can't believe Mom brought disposable diapers! Duh! Of course she brought disposable diapers! What is wrong with me?

A small child climbed into Mom's lap. My mother pulled a children's book from her handbag. Mom pointed to pictures and read a few pages. Except for the baby, the children crowded around Mom. She could have been a volunteer reader in any warm, well-lit library in North America.

Another child climbed into Mom's lap. Balancing a child on each thigh, she kept reading in French. Something she said made the children laugh. I wanted to enjoy the scene, but my mind felt jumbled. When I was little, my parents read hundreds of books to my brothers and me in what I thought was a humble abode. Now I pictured our little house and realized it was a palace.

I saw myself for what I was: a spoiled American. My stomach burned with shame. I couldn't wait to get out of there, but Mom seemed to be in no hurry.

"Piano lesson," I whispered to Mom. Glancing at her watch, she closed the book and stood up slowly, sliding each child to the floor.

"Mais, oui!" Mom cried. "J'ai presque oublié! Nous nous amusons quand nous lisons ensemble, n'est-ce pas?" The children nodded, understanding that Mom needed to get going and agreeing that it was fun to read together.

A chorus of "Au revoir!" saw us out the door. Mom and Sareeya paused as they whispered in the hallway. They squeezed each others' hands and kissed both cheeks.

We sat in the car. Mom made no move to turn the key.

"Where are the men?" I asked in a dull voice.

"The men are dead," Mom said quietly, confirming my suspicion. "Many Somalis have lost everything, Eveline. Everything. They've experienced things you wouldn't want to see in your worst nightmare."

My eyes filled with tears. "Mom," I said. "What's going to happen to the children?"

"The children . . . " Mom began. Pausing, she took a tissue from her purse. "The children are loved and cared for. Sareeya is the strongest person I've ever met. She'll carry those children, and Nadia, too, until they get where they need to go." Mom explained that the refugees, whom she'd met through Catholic Charities, awaited clearance to emigrate just a few miles north, to Canada. They were headed for my mother's home province of Québec, where the French language (if nothing else) was familiar.

Mom sighed. "Because of politics, I came here. Because of politics, they go there." She leaned her forehead on the steering wheel for a moment.

Lifting her head, she asked, "Do you know how many people were killed in the unrest in Québec that convinced Daddy and me to come here? I'm aware of one casualty. There may have been more, but when I heard about a man who died, I thought it was the worst thing in the world. So I try to imagine losing people I know—my whole family!"

I rolled down a window and felt refreshed by early December air.

"Eveline," Mom said, "our family is having a hard time. Dad is sick. But we are privileged. Don't forget that. Even with cancer and with Daddy out of work, even when I shop for groceries at midnight because I'm ashamed about being on food stamps during this hard time, the worst things that happen to us are nothing compared to what our friends have suffered."

Tears plopped onto my shirt.

Mom handed me a tissue. "I'm glad you had a good trip. It's important for you to have fun at this time in your life," she said, starting the car. "Now let's make the best of this day."

We drove back to the little house with chairs enough for all of us, and mattresses up on frames, covered with clean bedding. I stood in the kitchen while Mom taught a lesson in the next room. "Count, Alexander! Count!" The child fumbled with the easy Bach piece. "Try it again," Mom coaxed.

How do they do it? I wondered. *These strong women who carry everyone?*

Within a couple of years, my father died. Mom moved two Somali families into her home. After they emigrated to Canada, she took in a Syrian refugee.

I never took another road trip without thinking about refugees, political unrest, and my astounding privilege.

I have two things in common with Malala Yousafzai: I'm female, and I started speaking out about injustice as a pre-teen. The similarities end there.

I grew up in the quiet safety of northern New York and southern Québec. In contrast, Malala was raised in northwest Pakistan. At age twelve, I began touting the importance of feminism and my hopes for a world free of nuclear weapons. I suffered few repercussions beyond an occasional snide comment.

Malala advocated for the rights of girls to study and learn despite extremely high risks in a region pervaded by ideological extremists wanting to keep females hidden, submissive, and powerless.

I got a few dirty looks. Malala was shot in the head while on her school bus.

News of Malala's 2014 Nobel Peace Prize set me ablaze with inspiration. The indomitable teen's story lifted me, providing a hopeful contrast to dreary and alarming headlines. *What right have I to feel overwhelmed? If a child can remain steadfast, I must as well.*

Malala's Nobel acceptance speech inspired me to write a new song: "Malala, you stand fast for freedom!"

She told an interviewer she feels no bitterness toward her assailants.

"Your spirit, courageous and true!"

The young girl continued to speak her mind despite threats.

"Malala! Your voice was not silenced. You did not let violence stop you."

As I hummed the first few lines, I had no inkling the song would bring fifty singers and me into the presence of our young hero and her wonderful father. I'm grateful to longtime Amandla member Joan Featherman for alerting me to an announcement about Malala's US tour schedule, including a stop in Providence, Rhode Island, on July 28, 2016.

Our tour bus pulled up to the immense arena in Providence, Rhode Island, in line with instructions to arrive three hours before Malala's speech.

Singers looked astonished as we entered the massive place for our sound check. Our song sounded tiny in that cavernous room, but the technician adjusted levels until our voices filled the space. We prepared to present the song to thousands of Malala's fans just before her speech.

I learned, weeks earlier, that security would be extremely tight. "Don't get your hopes up about meeting Malala in person," an event coordinator warned. "If it's feasible, we'll bring her by your rehearsal room for a moment, but there's no guarantee."

After our sound check, the singers—aged nine to seventy-six—kept glancing at the door. Would we meet Malala or would we head back to Massachusetts without coming any closer than sitting in our arena seats and hearing her speak?

I cheered the singers and myself. "It would be enough, to sing the song and hear her speak!" I told them, although I harbored a fiery hope.

I wanted to give Malala a booklet I made for her featuring images of strong girls and decorated with our "Malala" song lyrics. During the bus ride, each singer had signed the booklet.

The chorus rehearsed the song until we couldn't bear to sing it again. We did yoga stretches, ate bagels, chugged water. We waited. Some singers lay on the floor. Many looked anxious.

We sang other songs loudly to blow off steam.

I suggested charades, which led to twenty minutes of hilarity. Yet the windowless room grew ever more stuffy. I felt like a weary schoolteacher after too many days of rain and not enough outdoor recess.

Still no Malala. My heart sank. *We've come all this way.*

An event coordinator appeared, out of breath. "She can't come here. But if you come right now, and believe me you have to sprint, you can meet her in the corridor for a few seconds. If you don't come right now, it'll be too late." He ran down the hall.

I surveyed the room strewn with water bottles, sheet music, sweaters, crumpled socks, bagel morsels. I looked at the kids, the elders, and everyone in between. *There's no way this will work.*

Yet they formed a tight group in an instant. Together, we ran. Singers with roots in India, Canada, Greece, Tibet, Puerto Rico, Germany, Poland, South Africa, Italy, the US, the UK, France, and Hungary sprinted as if our lives depended on it.

Men in suits and dark glasses stopped us as we approached the end of a corridor. Tiny wires snaked from their ears and disappeared under crisp collars. *Good Lord,* I thought, *we're in a spy movie.*

They ordered us to wait. The singers panted. We stood, confused, for five minutes. No one uttered a word.

The young woman wearing crimson rounded the corner followed by her smiling father. Singers inhaled sharply in one collective breath.

Malala looked quizzical as she surveyed our intergenerational crew in bright T-shirts and multi-colored sashes. I shook her hand

photo by Angie Gregory

Malala Yousafzai greets Eveline.

and her father's hand, then turned to the chorus and said, "Let's sing a bit of the song."

Hearing her name in the song's first word, Malala smiled. The half of her mouth that still moves easily turned up in delight. Despite her injuries, Malala is radiantly beautiful, glowing with intelligence and strength. Her father beamed.

When we switched from English to Urdu, father and daughter looked astonished. "Wow!" exclaimed Mr. Yousafzai, bringing both hands to his heart as tears sprang to his eyes.

Time was short, so I ended the song mid-chorus and handed Malala a bag of gifts, explaining there were presents for her brothers, as well.

She playfully scoffed, "Are you sure you want to give them presents?"

Everyone laughed.

Her dad stepped forward. "Malala, we should go on stage with them when they sing this wonderful song."

Malala nodded as producers and security staff scrambled to accommodate the new plan.

The singers received instructions to move swiftly through a labyrinthine backstage area and to stand in the wings during the introduction of our chorus and our song. Fifty of us received warnings to appear gracefully onstage without tripping on wires or falling on the narrow steps to the stage.

Next, we stood squinting under bright lights, trying to bring thousands of faces into focus.

We began singing as Malala and her dad remained offstage. Then, although we had not worked it out in advance, the pair stepped onstage just as we got to the words, "Millions of us cheer you on!"

In a frenzied standing ovation, wave after wave of gratitude rolled across the arena, swirled around the stage, and enveloped the young woman and her brave, progressive father.

When his firstborn arrived, Ziauddin Yousafzai broke with tradition by writing his daughter's name on the family tree, making her

Malala's dad, Ziauddin Yousafzai, greets Eveline.

the first female included in more than three hundred years of recorded history. There were no other daughters, mothers, sisters, grandmothers, or nieces listed. His groundbreaking act, for which he absorbed taunts, charted a new course.

Onstage, I watched delighted glances pass between father and daughter as we sang our hearts out in tribute.

Malala and Eveline with singers

The father vowed on the day of his daughter's birth that her wings would not be clipped. Inspired to find our own means of flight, we watch her soar.

No small thing

It's vital to keep things moving when performing for a large group of sixth graders. I knew I could lose them at any time and, once that slide begins, it's tough to reverse.

They're accustomed to video games rather than listening to a social-justice choir. I tried to keep it interesting. We sang a freedom song, read a short poem, and invited them to sing along with the next song. I refused to take it personally when some giggled or rolled their eyes. Most seemed grateful for a break in the day's routine, if nothing else.

"Our next song is 'Gabi Gabi' from South Africa," I announced. "Anyone know it?" I was joking, knowing that it's not exactly on the sixth grade hit parade. Yet a hand went up, belonging to a girl slumped in her chair in the back of the room.

After the program, kids surged toward the door. I caught up with the sad-looking girl who'd raised her hand. "Hi," I said. "I noticed you raised your hand. How do you know 'Gabi Gabi?'"

She mumbled, "I heard you last time. They held me back a year."

Her palpable shame reminded me of my own sixth grade year. I recalled not fitting in and wondering whether I'd survive being considered so weird. I watched the young girl's face harden until I thought it might crack.

"You remember that song even though you haven't heard us for a year? You have quite a memory!" I said, smiling.

Her gaze lifted a little, darting for a half-second of eye contact. She didn't exactly smile. It's more like she unfrowned.

"It's great to see you again," I said. With another dart of her eyes, she made a small sound and dashed out the door.

Soon, another girl appeared before me, bouncing with energy. "You remember me, right?" I did not but searched for clues. The daughter of a friend? A former student?

She wore glasses and braces. Her hair splayed in several cowlicks. Yet she exuded confidence with an unabashed smile. I did not detect a smidgen of shame. She awaited recognition. Buying time, I smiled back, trying to mirror her glow.

She announced, "I saw you last year at my other school! You were so great! Remember? I sat in the back row! You were great this year, too!"

I quickly answered, "Oh, yes! How nice to see you again!"

Giving me a big hug and a huge grin, she said, "It's great to see you!" and ran into the hallway jammed with kids.

When I was in sixth grade, a smart girl with glasses and awkward hair did not call attention to herself. Where did this one get her confidence?

What a contrast to the other girl. Still, the other one summoned the nerve to raise her hand, to risk standing out. That's no small thing. I hope she'll discover that each of us is born to shine, no matter how often we're held back.

Longing

My fascination with freedom songs in a wide variety of languages may spring from having an ancestral language overshadowed by shame. My experience is far less oppressive than others whose rich and deep cultural heritages are wrenched from them in violent ways. Compared with the experiences of most of humanity, my life is comfortable and fortunate. Yet I feel kinship with those separated from the rhythms and essences of their ancestors.

The French language inspires in me deep longing. Many Québécois people probably understand the complexity of my yearning.

I arrived June 26, 1964 in Ithaca, New York. My mother joyfully welcomed a girl, sister to the boy born in Québec City three years earlier. Céline gave birth to her second child in an alien place, attended by people whom she did not fully understand. Céline named me Eveline in honor of her mother, also born on the twenty-sixth day of June, in the year 1890 in a tiny Québécois village. She died seven years before my birth.

It's actually less than cosmic that I was born on my grandmother's birthday. My parents reluctantly moved to the US shortly before my birth, and Mom learned at the efficient American hospital that her new obstetrician planned to head out of town for a golf vacation. He would not postpone his trip for an impending birth. The doctor gave Céline two dates to choose from for induction. At the mercy of a foreign system, she struggled to understand his words and his reasoning.

She knew babies arrive when they're ready but didn't want to appear provincial. Signifying one of my mother's first lessons in her new land, she relented and chose June 26.

Stories about my parents' respective births illustrate differences in their backgrounds and help me understand more about my mother's startling experiences as a new immigrant.

My father entered the world in an efficient New York City hospital on May 2, 1932, one day after the official opening of the Empire State Building. In a metropolitan area buzzing with skyscraper excitement, the birth of little Robert Bruce — henceforth known by his middle name — didn't stand out for many citizens of his native Brooklyn. Yet for thirty-year-old Evelyn Parker MacDougall, an intellectual with no experience with children beyond teaching high school English, the arrival of her first child utterly changed life. Evelyn did not recall one moment of the anesthetized birth. She and my grandfather planned on having one child. Later, as they neared forty, the surprise arrival of twins turned their lives upside down.

A year after Bruce's arrival, Céline was born in a Québécois farmhouse, the last of eighteen pregnancies which resulted in ten live births. One might think they risked running out of names, but forty-two-year-old Eveline Rajotte Janelle and her husband Elphège named their last child Marie-Thérèse Françoise Céline Janelle.

My induced birth, a far cry from my mother's farmhouse arrival, nonetheless bore evidence of my mother's courage. Céline refused repeated offers of painkillers, afraid they might hurt the baby. My mother's thinking influenced my decision to give birth naturally forty years later. Similarly, Mom's insistence on nursing all of her babies despite exhortations to be modern and substitute formula led to choices I made when my own child arrived.

Following my birth in the US, Céline attempted to assimilate while retaining her own identity. This proved a tricky balancing act. My mother's relationship to her native tongue and roots became complex. Perhaps unavoidably, she handed the tangle off to my brothers and me. During the years my mother strove to learn English, we spoke little French at home. Yet when we drove a couple hours north to her home village, we heard only French and didn't want to be left out of games and gossip.

I sometimes tried to hide any hint of Frenchness to avoid American tormenters, yet I could immerse myself in Québécois culture when it suited me.

I recall sitting on my parents' bed watching my mother pack for an extended trip with my father to Europe. They planned to work with a musical group and she admonished me to look after Ian, my baby brother, while my siblings and I stayed with relatives in Québec. One piece of advice, a refrain I heard over the years, confused me: "Don't speak like them, up there."

How does she expect me to live up there but not speak like them? Mom cringed at what she perceived as rejections of Québécois culture and language. She took those slights (perceived or real) very personally, yet she also engaged in putdowns. I grew up with a curious mix of messages.

Even in adulthood, I often feel tongue-tied when speaking French with someone I don't know. Yet it brings me great joy to converse with my cousins, to read articles in French, and to listen to French news over the internet.

I long to live in a world where every person respects the histories and cultures of others. What a person speaks is language, not dialect. What a person wears is clothing, not costume. We could solve scores of serious problems if we learn to celebrate, recognize and honor instead of shaming, judging, and denigrating. Will humanity ever get it?

why keep doing it?

If something makes sense to me, I do it. If it doesn't, I skip it or stop. Sometimes, I go in one direction for a while but come to feel that it ceases to make sense. I'm a work in progress.

The fact that something makes sense to me doesn't mean I expect others to feel the same. Similarly, I don't embark on conventional paths unless they suit me. I don't go out of my way to be different. It just seems to come naturally.

At age twenty-five, I worked in Deerfield with Wally Nelson on a Friday afternoon preparing produce for the Saturday farmers' market in Greenfield. We worked that way every week, weighing and bundling vegetables while Juanita worked on other projects like gathering baskets, figuring prices, and readying the truck.

On Fridays, we hit the hay exhausted from a sixteen-hour day, knowing we would rise at dawn.

At times, Wally and I kept up a steady stream of conversation. At other times, we worked silently. On that June day, I felt troubled by a personal concern and broke the silence with a question.

"Wally? How did you know beyond the shadow of a doubt that Juanita was the one for you?" I knew they had challenging times when they first got together, but their track record of forty-plus years convinced me they were inseparable.

Wally finished bundling carrots, saying, "We work it out every day."

I laughed.

He picked up a loose carrot. Pointing it at me, he asked, "You think I'm kidding?" His stern expression sobered me.

I asked, "Are you saying you don't feel one hundred percent certain about your relationship with Juanita?" I wanted some things in this world be immutable, and I counted on the Nelsons' relationship to be one of those things.

I added, "Is this too personal?"

"No," Wally replied, "It's not too personal. You're family. Listen: the time to make big decisions about your life is every single morning, when you wake up. Take a good look at your life and ask questions. Find some good answers before breakfast."

I digested that piece of wisdom. Wally began to chuckle. I glanced at his face and saw a twinkle in his eye, all sternness gone.

"Every morning, I wake up next to Nita and ask myself whether she's the one. The answer comes to me: Yes, definitely. So far, it's working out pretty good."

He drew out "pretty good" in his thickest Arkansas drawl. I mimicked him until we cracked up. I howled, relieved to blow off steam.

The screen door creaked open. Juanita demanded, "What the Sam Hell is going on out here? You two don't have plenty of work?"

Wally and I rolled our eyes, starting a new batch of giggles. "Hi Sweetie-Pie," Wally called out. "I'm just telling Ever-leen that you're the sweetest, loveliest woman who's ever lived, and I'm danged lucky to wake up with you each day!"

Nita responded haughtily, "I get better with time, Mister, believe me. Better with time." The screen door slammed again. I heard Nita chuckling from inside the house.

We got back to work. Wally's words of wisdom and our collective mirth made the work go by quickly, giving me guiding principles I've tried to follow ever since.

Jane Sapp

Jane Sapp changes the energy in any room where she puts her hands to a piano and begins to sing. As I introduced her at Northampton's Edwards Church on March 23, 2019, I tried to express adequately the depth of my appreciation for a phenomenal teacher and mentor. I told the audience,

Jane Sapp

> I performed with Jane in '89 and '90 to spotlight issues related to apartheid in South Africa and here at home. A seasoned gospel singer, educator, and community organizer, Jane taught me a great deal when I was just starting out as a director.

When I reflect on attributes I've admired in my mentors, I recognize that Jane embodies them all. She possesses Nelson Mandela's quality of clear, compassionate leadership. Like Malala Yousafzai, Jane courageously advocates for education.

Dr. Horace Clarence Boyer made gospel music the center of his life's work.

Jane's lifelong relationship to gospel music has inspired countless people all over the world.

Wally and Juanita Nelson walked their talk. Jane does that every day. Pete Seeger's passionate activism through music moved people across generations, a gift that Jane also possesses. When I think of Archbishop Desmond Tutu's wisdom and sense of humor, and how he intertwines the two, I recognize that Jane also possesses those qualities.

A fan recently noted, "You started the chorus when you were so young!"

I chuckled and replied, "Jane Sapp directed not one but two choirs by the time she was twelve! She engages people of all ages in singing traditional and contemporary songs, including her own compositions. She encourages young people to create songs, too, which she helps polish into gems."

We're celebrating the publication of Jane's new book, *Let's Make a Better World.* Please help me welcome . . .

As I said her name, the audience exploded in thunderous applause, blossoming to a standing ovation before she'd even sung her first song. Thirty years after my first show with Jane, I had the privilege of sharing the stage with her again, and by lucky coincidence, it occurred during the special concert where our chorus announced our new name, Fiery Hope.

For someone so skilled in performing, Jane carries herself with genuine humility, the kind that gently announces, "This is who I am. This is what I offer. I change everything around me simply by being myself." In a world cluttered with performers motivated by ego, Jane demonstrates that collaborative work, not personalities, should be the focus.

The preceding October, Kate Stevens, a social-justice activist and retired minister, asked if I would help organize events during Jane's visit to the Northeast the following spring. I leapt at the chance to see Jane again.

Kate and I met with our co-conspirator, Jenny Ladd, a Northampton-based organizer, and pored over congested calendars to find times and places to feature Jane in the Pioneer Valley. Possibilities seemed elusive. Then I saw the little calendar square representing March 23, the evening Amandla would present a spring concert where we planned to announce our new name.

"We could include Jane in our Northampton show," I said, "but I already have an opening act, and it's our major spring concert, so I worry about not being able to give her the time she deserves." Kate noted that Jane wasn't looking for a feature spot and would probably appreciate going easy on her voice during a busy tour.

It turned out Jane could appear with us on March 23. Some of my chorus members were unfamiliar with her work, but once they heard her recording of "Movin' On," they were all in.

Sometimes, the stars line up beautifully. It happened when fourteen-year-old Gillis got suspended for walking out of school with many of his peers to protest the influence exerted in the US by the pro-gun lobby. Normally, suspension does not fill a parent with pride, but I applauded my son after he decided, entirely without my input, to participate in the action. He and many of his schoolmates walked the mile to Greenfield town common and held signs, shared speeches, and stood together for sanity and genuine forms of safety. It's a convoluted issue in some ways, yet in other ways it's pretty simple.

Gillis's suspension allowed him to accompany me to Northampton the morning Jane and I were guests on Bill Newman's popular WHMP radio show. Gillis listened intently as we sat with Jane in the waiting room before going on the air. She shared stories of working with people in the rural South on issues of civil rights, voter registration, and other vital projects. Gillis took it all in as Jane shared vignettes about African Americans who experience ridicule, abuse, and death at the hands of some police officers. Even though we'd heard such stories before, hearing them first-hand from Jane felt additionally sobering.

Meeting Jane in my mid twenties impacted me immensely, but at that time in my life, I lacked deep understanding about many issues. Working with her again in my mid fifties inspired me to keep learning and, above all, to keep working for justice. With Jane as a model, I know I will never give up. We've got to keep "movin' on!"

Eveline and Jane Sapp accept applause with
Fiery Hope singers after its March 23, 2019 concert in Northampton.
Jane's husband, Hubert, holds a floral tribute.

Fiery Hope

I generally keep our chorus events to about ninety minutes, but our March 23, 2019 concert in Northampton exceeded two hours. The show took on a life of its own due to a confluence of blessings.

Before learning of Jane Sapp's availability, I had invited Burikes, six young adults performing material from Eastern Europe and the Balkans, to open our show. Burikes means beets in Yiddish, and the band serves up joyful sustenance like a bunch of deeply colorful root vegetables.

I met one of the members of Burikes, Sadie Gold-Shapiro, when she was four years old and her mom, Joanne, joined Amandla. Sadie grew up in our chorus. After graduating from Smith College and traveling the world, Sadie headed back to western Massachusetts and joined our chorus. When I heard a clip of her band, I knew I wanted to spotlight the talented young folks.

I'd also chosen March 23 to announce that we would change the name of the chorus from Amandla to Fiery Hope. When I learned that Jane could be with us, as well, I knew the evening would be very full and the audience would be invited on a journey of reflection, determination, and joy.

A week before the show, a newspaper reporter asked: "Isn't it hard to change your name after thirty years?"

"Not really," I replied. "What feels hard is learning to dismantle white supremacy because it seems as if there are two kinds: virulently vicious and another sort that's perceived by some white people as more benign. But I don't understand how an ideology that kills people and depletes communities can be seen as acceptable."

During the concert, I told the audience that, when our chorus began in 1988, we worked alongside our South African sisters and brothers to raise awareness about the crushing system of apartheid in their beautiful, troubled land. A South African member suggested the name Amandla for our singing group, since the Zulu word for power appears in many South African freedom songs.

In 1988, I found it easier to recognize South African racism than to acknowledge the many forms of toxic apartheid here in the US, right under my nose. My learning curve will continue for the rest of my life as I attempt to recognize and disavow the racism I've ingested along with American television, magazines, movies, schooling, government, religion, economics, and many other categories and institutions.

I explained to the audience that—as the South African political landscape changed in the early nineties following Nelson Mandela's release from decades in prison and after his election as President—things changed for our chorus, as well. Many South Africans with whom we'd sung and worked headed back home to take up positions of leadership. At the same time, Amandla broadened our repertoire to include songs of struggle and justice from around the world, including the US.

The thought occurred to me over the years that a name change might someday be in order, given that I'm a white woman directing a chorus with an African name, but the shift seemed overwhelming, and it felt easier to turn away from the thought.

It wasn't until a 2018 conversation with members of the Greenfield-based Racial Justice Rising group that I knew the time had come. For months, our singers suggested and voted on dozens of possibilities, with Fiery Hope emerging as the overall favorite. I suggested that name because of what happened in the moment when I met Malala Yousafzai and her dad in 2016. As I shook their hands, the words "fiery hope" popped into my mind and have stayed with me ever since.

I tried to keep my remarks brief at the Northampton concert, but I didn't want to minimize the significance of our group's transition, especially as white supremacy gained more toeholds in our culture, from the White House on down.

After I delivered my statement, the show went on. But something stuck in my craw . . . something I didn't recognize until Jane's solo set.

Gillis sometimes expresses disgust that "grown-ups don't take things seriously. They're leaving a huge mess." He cites gun policy, civil rights injustices, climate crises, and other systemic problems. I try to point out examples of inspiring activism but have to acknowledge that our culture is rife with complacency.

I've talked with my child about racial disparities and the importance of reparations in a culture loaded with slavery's legacies. Nudged by his reminder that talk is cheap, I try to find ways to act, too.

As a lifelong tax resister, my objections go far beyond bloated military budgets and misguided priorities. I resist the tentacles of white supremacy that have twisted US public policy for centuries. Our nation did not simply take a few wrong turns—as some suggest—it's built on rotten foundations. The Declaration of Independence and the Constitution contain lofty ideals and important words, but as a society, we have not yet succeeded in living up to those ideals. Not until freedoms extend to everyone will we live in truly united states.

Reading lists at Gillis's progressive public school include works by Ronald Takaki, Howard Zinn, Isabel Wilkerson, Ta-nehisi Coates, and Jill Lapore. Students and teachers engage in lively discussion and direct action. When I volunteer and substitute teach at the school, I hear teens' perspectives and find myself moved by their passion and clarity.

At the concert, the power of Jane's songs triggered in me an urgent desire to do more. In one achingly beautiful song, she sang, "Please, be patient with me." Though gentle, the song nudged me to work harder in our troubled world.

I consistently earn under taxable levels, yet even if I did owe tax dollars, I would not be able to give my money to our violence-driven government. I will be happy to pay when priorities change.

Yet at the same time, I benefit from living in this nation, like when I drive on paved highways. I also know that others depend on funding that supports education, housing, transportation, health, and veterans' benefits, among other things. My choices are imperfect as I navigate the many conundrums of life in the US.

In trying to balance what I contribute with how I benefit, each year I volunteer with community projects and donate approximately five percent of my gross income to non-profit organizations.

The beauty and depth of Jane's music that evening inspired me to earmark my annual contribution to one or two organizations of her choice. As she continued singing, my heart opened further until I decided to increase my donation to match the traditional tithing rate of ten percent.

Of nearly twenty-thousand dollars, I calculated, that comes to about two thousand dollars. As I watched my son take in Jane's music and wisdom, I realized that I needed to do something, and to do it publicly, that very evening.

When Jane finished her last solo song, I gestured to chorus members that, yes, we were about to sing with her, but I wanted them to hold on a minute. Accustomed to my spontaneity, they settled in to their seats once more.

I approached the microphone on shaky legs. "We'll do a couple of songs with Jane to close the show, but first, I want to ask my son to come up here."

I'll never know for certain whether it was appropriate to speak publicly of my impulse. A wealthy white woman later said, "You made it about you, not about the chorus. I felt really uncomfortable." Perhaps she was right. But an opening line from a David Whyte essay rang in my ears — something about work being intimate, "the place where the self meets the world."

Before the microphone, I swallowed hard and realized that parenting with intention is perhaps more important than everything else I do, combined.

Several people later told me they disapproved of the fact that I publicly shared with Gillis my plan to double my donation that year. As Gillis stood next to me at the microphone, I touched the skin on his face. "If you were brown-skinned, I would be terrified every time you step outside my door in these United States. But because you're this color, I don't worry too much. Many parents do worry, though, every moment about the safety of their black and brown children, and it shouldn't be like that. Let's think of ways to help make it right."

My son looked deep into my eyes and nodded. *He gets it.* My heart nearly burst.

People who criticized my statement that evening were older as well as white or wealthy or both. A larger number of people who let me know they appreciated my remarks were younger as well as of lower income, people of color, or both.

I received a message the next day from Jane. She used the word "courage" to describe my remarks to Gillis.

I'm not sure how courageous it was. For white Americans, it's easy to participate in events and meetings while continuing to enjoy favored status. I made my statement in a public way in order to challenge myself, and to do so in front of my son who wonders "whether adults give a s−t." I also wanted to challenge others. We'll never get anywhere if we wait for governments to bring change. We've got to get the ball rolling ourselves.

While I'm not wealthy, I am white, so I automatically have a pocket full of cultural coupons. I feel drawn to voluntary simplicity and to make reparations wherever I can, recognizing that my choices are blessings, not sacrifices.

I asked Jane to recommend organizations so I might split my donation between two of her favorites. She chose the Encampment for Citizenship and the Southern Partners Fund. Before mailing the checks, I asked Gillis if he'd like to add his name to the cover letters. I described each organization and explained they were Jane's top picks.

Children of the digital age are more accustomed to using keyboards than writing implements, but for this occasion, Gillis reached for a pen and even used cursive with pride to sign each letter.

After a couple of people suggested that I'd done Gillis a disservice by "putting him on the spot," I asked my son how he felt.

"Why are they concerned about that, when they could be concerned about the planet?" he noted, adding, "I've grown up in front of audiences. It's not a big deal."

I resonate with the maxim "Not to decide, is to decide." Similarly, I believe it's irresponsible to raise a white boy without teaching him about racial, economic, and other kinds of disparities. To raise a white child without radical cultural understanding is to risk inflicting upon the world another entitled white supremacist. We have plenty of those already.

I don't regret what I said to my son that evening nor where I said it. By caring about justice, he teaches me what I need to do.

Afterword: why we sing

adapted from my November 26, 2016, column in the **Greenfield Recorder**

The tumultuous election cycle of 2016 left most of us exhausted. Never before have I witnessed such rancor or recriminations. The morning after the election, I switched on the radio to learn whether we had President Clinton or President Trump. I knew that, either way, most Americans would not feel truly happy.

In the constant barrage of our era's tweets and scandals, people try to adjust to a new normal. No matter our political affiliation, many of us wonder about how to survive on our beleaguered planet.

As I try to keep my balance as a choral director, a mom, and a citizen of the planet, I'm spurred on by stories about some of my heroes.

During the 1940s, young Wally Nelson and a few other activists entered a diner to protest segregation. The owner — a large, volatile man in cook's garb — screamed so loudly that customers vacated instantly. The enraged man bellowed that he would fetch a meat cleaver and, upon his return, chop anyone he found into pieces.

The would-be protestors vanished — except for Wally. The angry cook returned wielding a cleaver and rushed to Wally with the razor-sharp tool held high.

In a quiet, steady voice, Wally said, "Friend, you don't know what you're doing." The cleaver froze above the man's reddened face. He stared at Wally, taking in that dignified, calm, five-foot, three-inch man with "beautiful brown skin" (as Wally was famous for saying).

For what was likely five or ten seconds — but which to Wally felt like an hour — the man was paralyzed with wonder. He slowly lowered the cleaver and released it, clattering, to the floor. He murmured, "You're right. I don't know what I'm doing" and slowly walked back to the kitchen, head down.

Wally eased out the door. His friends slipped from hiding places, saying, "Man, we thought we'd never see you again!"

I heard Wally tell that story in many settings. He reminded people of all ages not to be fooled into turning another person into The Other, even if they act like your enemy. "That's when we become our own enemy," he chided.

My friendship with Wally and Juanita Nelson showed me that humans can solve problems in astonishingly creative ways.

When I held the strong, soft hand of Malala Yousafzai, I reflected on her assertion that she feels no anger toward the men who shot her in the head. In the face of her courage, who am I to waste energy on despair when it's needed for hard work?

When I looked into the eyes of Malala's dad, I saw a man who has spent years with a target on his back. He nearly lost his daughter, he's lost his home, yet he moves forward with hope and grace.

In 1990, Nelson Mandela grinned at our chorus members and said, "Yes, let's sing!" He'd been in prison longer than I'd been alive. He spent twenty-seven years separated from loved ones, forced into hard labor, and stripped of rights — but never of dignity.

Archbishop Desmond Tutu nodded in 1992 as we belted out "Nkosi Sikelel' iAfrika" for an audience of two thousand. Before and after our appearance onstage, his infectious laugh left me grinning despite the gravity of the topics at hand. It's hard to reconcile his joy with his life history, but if he can laugh, certainly I can carry on.

Pete Seeger lost jobs during the McCarthy era and wondered how on earth he'd support his family. Despair was tempting, but he kept singing, speaking up for justice, and listening to people. Over the years, I asked him, "Does music really make a difference?"

He reassured me every time, "It's often the only thing that does. Don't ever quit."

When I wonder how to get through the next moment, I feel guided by folks who persevere in the face of steep odds. I reach for my pitch pipe, smile at the singers, and give the starting notes. This is how I travel the world.

acknowledgments from Eveline

Though I grew up in a musical family, I received no formal training as a choral director. For me, every day means on-the-job training. The heartfelt support of hundreds of singers and thousands of fans over the years inspires me to continue learning about directing, writing and arranging music, and engaging as an activist.

Most singers with whom I've worked had no formal musical training. Some took music lessons in childhood, and several earned college-level music degrees. But the majority want to make a difference in the world by singing with others, and they work hard to achieve that goal. To all current and former chorus members: thank you for practicing individually, rehearsing with the group, traveling to events, and performing. It's hard work to change the world one song at a time. You enrich my life and our communities, beyond measure.

I'm especially grateful to patient members in the early years. At times, I experienced steep learning curves as I grew up alongside the chorus. Many of you helped guide me.

I feel grateful to each of the people who appear in my stories and accounts. I will not repeat their names here, but I'm indebted to each one.

How I wish I could include an exhaustive list of everybody who helped me start and sustain the chorus, but that list might double the size of this volume. Scores of chorus members, fans, and supporters assisted me in dozens of ways.

I feel deeply grateful to those who attended steering committee and board meetings, sewed sashes, organized boxes of sheet music, volunteered as bookkeepers, coordinated travel, recorded rehearsals, designed graphics, built and maintained our website, served as section leaders, translated or did linguistic research and—perhaps most important—offered ears and hearts when I needed sounding boards in the complex business of leading diverse, multi-generational groups in scenarios by turns joyful and stressful but never, ever dull.

I knew Marcia Gagliardi of Haley's for many years as an acquaintance, and one of my luckiest breaks occurred when I ran into her at the food co-op just as I began thinking of writing a book. My acquaintance became my publisher, and my publisher ultimately became one of my dearest friends. Marcia, thank you.

People in my irrepressible, large tribe have influenced me and shaped our world with outrageous creativity and spunk. Last names include MacDougall, Janelle, Rajotte, Fluet, St. Onge, Bourgeouis, and really, about half of the province of Québec. I'm grateful to each one.

To my two dearest fellows in the world, Douglas and Gillis, I give my deepest thanks.

About the author

At the age of twenty-three in 1988, Eveline MacDougall founded the Amandla Chorus, known as Fiery Hope since 2019. She works at a wide variety of jobs to support her love of learning about the world one song at a time. In addition to being a choral director, she's a fiddler, substitute teacher, housecleaner, and itinerant visual artist. She believes that being a parent should garner more respect in our culture than being an overpaid CEO. She lives in western Massachusetts.

photo by Paul Franz

Eveline MacDougall

Text and captions for *Fiery Hope* are set in Book Antiqua, a Microsoft roman typeface based on pen-drawn letters of the Italian Renaissance. Because it is distinctive and gentle in appearance, it can be used to give a document a different feeling than that given by the more geometrical designs of most text faces. Its beautiful italic has many uses.

Eveline MacDougall designed title art and text breakers.

CPSIA information can be obtained
at www.ICGtesting.com
Printed in the USA
JSHW021242140220
4229JS00003B/8

9 781948 380102